CARE PACKAGES
FOR YOUR
CUSTOMERS

CARE PACKAGES
FOR YOUR
CUSTOMERS

An Idea a Week to Enhance Customer Service

Barbara A. Glanz
CSP

McGraw-Hill

New York   Chicago   San Francisco   Lisbon   London
Madrid   Mexico City   Milan   New Delhi
San Juan   Seoul   Singapore   Sydney   Toronto

The *McGraw·Hill* Companies

1 2 3 4 5 6 7 8 9 0   FGR/FGR   0 9 8 7

ISBN-13: 978-0-07-148421-3
ISBN-10: 0-07-148421-3

McGraw-Hill books are available at special discounts to use as premiums and sales promotions, or for use in corporate training programs. For more information, please write to the Director of Special Sales, Professional Publishing, McGraw-Hill, Two Penn Plaza, New York, NY 10121-2298. Or contact your local bookstore.

Library of Congress Cataloging-in-Publication Data

Glanz, Barbara A.
  Care packages for your customers / by Barbara Glanz.
     p. cm.
  Includes index.
  ISBN 0-07-148421-3 (alk. paper)
  1. Customer loyalty. 2. Customer services. 3. Customer relations.
  I. Title.

HF5415.5.G548 2007
658.8'12—dc22   2006036390

*This book is dedicated
to all my precious customers
who have believed in me and my message and
to each person out there who is making
his or her customers feel special.
Thank you for CARE-ing!*

Contents

Acknowledgments

My deepest appreciation goes to my dear friends, Ken and Shannon Johnston, the founders of Kaset International, a company which focused solely on customer service training, consulting, and measurement. They believed in me and offered me a job as their manager of training when I was just returning to the workforce after raising my three children. Their wisdom, experience, and focus on service gave me the foundation and the passion to do the speaking and writing I have done over the past 11 years. They are the giants upon whose shoulders I stood to reach the place where I am today.

I also thank all my wonderful clients worldwide who have embraced my message and have so willingly shared both their pain and their success stories. They have allowed me to "spread my contagious enthusiasm" throughout their organizations, and the result has been a blessing to both employees and customers alike.

I especially want to thank my dear friend, John McPherson, the creator of the cartoon strip "Close to Home," for always being willing to let me share his warm and funny cartoons with all my audiences. His amazing talent is matched only by his generosity and huge and loving heart. Thank you, John! You can reach him at closetohome@mac.com or www.closetohome.

Finally, I want to thank Donya Dickerson, my very special editor, who has believed in this project from the start. I only hope that you, my readers, will find ideas which will help your organization better serve all human beings, both internally and externally, who so desperately need acceptance, purpose, and caring in this hurting world.

The Clerk
With The Smirk

The shop it was busy.
The clerk he was not.
The more shoppers asked him,
The dumber he got.

"They don't pay me enough,
To do all this work."
"They don't pay me enough,"
Said the Clerk With the Smirk.

"Slow, slower, slowest:
That's my strategy.
You want it done fast,
Don't try asking me."

"I hate working here. . . .
All irk and no perk.
I long to get axed,"
Said the Clerk With the Smirk.

"I'll be unemployed.
I'll go on the dole.
No taxes to pay,
No rigamarole."

And the Clerk With the Smirk
Soon got himself fired.
The boss sent him packing,
With language inspired.

Thought the Clerk With the Smirk,
"That's fine, fine, fine.
I'll collect unemployment;
I'll go get in line."

But the lines there were long,
And the service so poor,
That waiting and waiting
Became quite a chore.

At last at the front,
The smirker did whine,
"The help here is lousy.
You ought to resign."

The man sized him up,
And said with a sneer,
"I'm closing this line;
You can go to the rear."

"Hey, wait, No you don't!"
Cried the Clerk With the Smirk.
"I'll see that you're fired
For the work that you shirk."

To the Clerk With the Smirk
Said the Clerk With the Sneer,
"Thanks to people like you,
I'll always be here."

Preface

Most organizations today have discovered that rarely do they have a unique product or service. Therefore, their only differentiator is the level of service they give to their customers. They spend hundreds of thousands of dollars and dozens of hours on customer service training, and yet once the training has ended it is difficult to keep that spirit of service over self-interest alive and well. Over and over again, my clients have asked me for a resource to help them to continually inspire and motivate their employees to give exceptional service without having to spend more time in a classroom.

This book is written for anyone who is involved with customers, whether you are a frontline employee, a supervisor, or a manager and whether you have external or internal customers. It is filled with ideas that you can use to keep the spirit of service alive in your organization and that will encourage you to give the best of yourself to your work—in many low-cost or no-cost ways.

Since 1988, when I began my return career after raising three children, I have been working in one way or another in customer service. I have trained thousands of people all over the world, spoken to hundreds of organizations about service, and written six books on the topic, so I feel well qualified to write this book. My deepest passion is helping people to understand how just one person can make a difference to create loyal customers for life, and that one person can be *you*.

From 1988 to 1994, I was Manager of Training and Director of Quality in Training for Kaset International, a Times Mirror firm dedicated to enhancing customer service in organizations all over the world. Here, I learned the nuts and bolts of customer service training, the skills one needs to succeed. However, I discovered that skills alone are not enough. One must have a *heart* for service in order to make a difference every day.

I began to explore ways to make extraordinary service come alive, first focusing on what the organization could do. My first book in 1993 was titled in the first edition *The Creative Communicator: 399 Ways to Communicate Commitment Without Boring People to Death!*, and it focused on creative ways to communicate an organization's commitment to customer service, what today we might call "branding" or a combination of public relations (PR) and marketing with a service focus.

Then I began talking to customers themselves. My second book in 1994, *Building Customer Loyalty: How YOU Can Help Keep Customers Returning*, was based on research with hundreds of people all across America, asking them if they were loyal to any organization and, if so, why. In almost every case they told us a story about one employee who created an experience that dazzled them. Thus, it was proven to me that customer loyalty is truly created person by person and experience by experience. Outstanding customer service is about both a **relationship** and a **memory**!

In 1995 I left Kaset to start my own company, Barbara Glanz Communcations, Inc., because I realized that just customer service training was not enough to ensure dazzling service day by day. In my research I discovered a critical truth: *Employees will never treat customers any better than they are being treated themselves.* As a result, I wanted to focus on supporting and encouraging both organizations and employees to create an *atmosphere* that would support extraordinary service. I began to speak all over the world on how to create workplaces that would encourage and allow people to give great service.

Two of my subsequent books, *CARE Packages for the Workplace: Dozens of Little Things You Can Do to Regenerate Spirit at Work* and *Handle with CARE: Motivating and Retaining Employees*, used the metaphor of CARE Packages to describe how to create an environment that supports, encourages, and celebrates excellent service. These books include many ideas of how to treat customers internally and externally to create positive memorable customer experiences.

My latest book, coauthored with Ken Blanchard, *The Simple Truths of Service Inspired by Johnny the Bagger*, shares stories of ordinary people in ordinary jobs who are making an extraordinary difference. It tells heartwarming stories and inspires people with the *hope* that they *can* make a difference, which is the first step (desire) in creating extraordinary service. However, it does not contain ideas to reinforce a daily focus on giving extraordinary service, so that is the purpose of *CARE Packages for Your Customers*.

This book, more than any other, emphasizes in a practical, immediately implementable way the basic beliefs I have come to have about service:

- *You cannot mandate it.* You cannot threaten, cajole, or reward enough to ensure great service. Rather, it must come from the inside out, from the heart. Employees must *want* to give good service, not for the organization or for the boss but because it is the right thing to do and it gives purpose and meaning to their work. It is a behavior that you choose.

- *Great customer service is all about an experience.* It is not something tangible that you can quantify or measure; instead, it is about how people feel in that interaction. Great service always leaves the customers feeling better because they interacted with a person, even if they did not get exactly what they wanted. They feel like someone CAREs about them as human beings.

- *About 80 percent of good customer service involves creative, out-of-the-box thinking.* It focuses on what an employee *can* do, not what they can't do, always offering options and creative ideas for solutions. The employee may not be able to do exactly what the customer wants, but he or she can always empathize with the customer on the human level and then creatively explore the options of what can be done on the business level.

- *For most people, the emphasis on service needs to be constantly at the forefront of everything they do.* We are all highly stressed in our workplaces today, and there are many demands on our time, so we need constant reminders of how important and how simple one-on-one customer service really is.

So, great customer service *is* simple. It revolves around the letters in the acronym CARE, the elements of a spirited, service-oriented organization:

C = **C**reative **C**ommunication

A = **A**tmosphere and **A**ppreciation for **A**ll

R = **R**espect and **R**eason for Being

E = **E**mpathy and **E**nthusiasm

In this book you will find one idea a week to inspire, support, and encourage you—and, if you are a manager, your employees—to give extraordinary service, both to internal and external customers. Use it as a resource for weekly inspiration and for ideas to improve your work as well as how you feel about your job. If you are a manager, it is an excellent resource for staff meetings. The book can be used as a management or supervisory tool, or it can be used simply as a stimulator for your own creative ideas.

May your life and work always be filled with CARE!

Blessings,

Barbara

6140 Midnight Pass Road #802
Sarasota, FL 34242
941-312-9169; Fax 941-349-8209
bglanz@barbaraglanz.com
www.barbaraglanz.com

Introduction

SELF ASSESSMENT— HOW WELL ARE YOU CURRENTLY DOING IN BUILDING CUSTOMER LOYALTY?

▶ **THE IDEA**

Building customer loyalty is the responsibility of every employee in an organization. If organizations today want to stay in business in the private sector, they must do more than simply acquire new customers. They must treat their customers in such a way that the customers *want* to do more business with the organization. Likewise, in the public sector, citizens will no longer put up with poor treatment and inefficient service. Those departments in government that are not willing to provide good service to their citizen-customers are slowly becoming privatized, and their employees are finding themselves out of jobs. So, in every organization, whether it is in the public or private sector, each individual employee must be responsible for creating loyal customers.

► THE IDEA IN ACTION

Many years of research have shown that there are certain behaviors that create customer loyalty. Use this self-assessment to see how well you are currently building customer loyalty in your organization.

1. I know my products well, and I always try to teach my customer a little more about my organization's products or services.

   Almost Always   Sometimes   Almost Never

2. I offer my customers options and alternatives so that they may make a wise decision.

   Almost Always   Sometimes   Almost Never

3. I explain all information, especially answers to their concerns and questions, carefully, fully, and respectfully.

   Almost Always   Sometimes   Almost Never

4. I do things for my customers even when it is "not my job" to do them.

   Almost Always   Sometimes   Almost Never

5. I take personal responsibility to solve a customer's problem. I don't simply dump it on someone else.

   Almost Always   Sometimes   Almost Never

6. I routinely follow up with several of my customers each week to see if they are happy with our products or services.

   Almost Always   Sometimes   Almost Never

7. I learn my customers' names whenever possible, and I use their names at least once in a conversation. I also tell them my name and spell it for them if necessary.

   Almost Always   Sometimes   Almost Never

8. I remember customers' names when they return to my place of work.

   Almost Always   Sometimes   Almost Never

9. I work at noticing something special about each person or listening for personal information they might share. Then I refer to this information at some time in our conversation.

   Almost Always   Sometimes   Almost Never

10. I am willing to bend the rules for my customers.

    Almost Always   Sometimes   Almost Never

11. I am willing to give up some personal time (breaks, lunchtime, at the end of my shift) when the customer needs it.

    Almost Always   Sometimes   Almost Never

12. I often do something extra to "surprise" and please my customers.

    Almost Always   Sometimes   Almost Never

13. I treat every customer as if he or she was my friend or neighbor, and I try to put myself in his or her shoes.

    Almost Always   Sometimes   Almost Never

14. I take a sincere personal interest in my customers—their families, their jobs, their needs. I work hard at remembering special things about them, and I inquire about these things when I talk with them again.

    Almost Always   Sometimes   Almost Never

15. I really listen to my customers' needs and feelings; then I act on what I hear.

    Almost Always   Sometimes   Almost Never

16. When either I make a mistake or my organization makes a mistake, I apologize sincerely to the customer, and I do my very best to fix it. Then I do something extra for that customer.

    Almost Always   Sometimes   Almost Never

17. I often make suggestions of other things we can do to help the customer. If I or my organization cannot, with creative think-

ing, solve a customer's problem, I will recommend another source, perhaps even a competitor.

Almost Always   Sometimes   Almost Never

18. I trust my customers and always assume that their intentions are honest.

Almost Always   Sometimes   Almost Never

19. When helping a customer, I always express my thanks and appreciation to them for choosing our organization.

Almost Always   Sometimes   Almost Never

20. I always treat the customer with respect, making the customer feel more important than I or my organization.

Almost Always   Sometimes   Almost Never

21. I stay calm and respectful even with a customer who is arguing with me.

Almost Always   Sometimes   Almost Never

22. I empathize with the customers' concerns, even if I do not agree with them. I use listening skills to acknowledge customers' feelings and show them that I care.

Almost Always   Sometimes   Almost Never

23. Even when the customers are not there, I do what is best for them, not what is easiest or fastest for me.

Almost Always   Sometimes   Almost Never

24. I am creative in thinking of ways I can add my personal signature to my work and delight my customers.

Almost Always   Sometimes   Almost Never

25. I follow through as quickly as possible when I make a promise to a customer. This includes returning phone calls within 24 hours.

Almost Always   Sometimes   Almost Never

26. I ask clear, appropriate questions to clarify or gather the additional information I need to be sure I fully understand a customer's situation.

Almost Always   Sometimes   Almost Never

27. Even in the midst of confusion, long lines, phones ringing, emergencies, and constant other interruptions, I stay calm and treat each customer with friendliness, courtesy, and patience.

Almost Always   Sometimes   Almost Never

28. I smile a lot and share how much I enjoy my job and my customers.

Almost Always   Sometimes   Almost Never

▶ TIPS FOR IMPLEMENTATION

Look at those behaviors you have marked "Almost Never." These are the first ones you need to focus on improving. Then examine those you marked "Sometimes." You may want to discuss these items with your manager or your team so that you will find it easier to do these things most of the time. Then congratulate yourself on those behaviors you checked "Almost Always," If you scored more "Sometimes" and "Almost Always," you are on your way to building customer loyalty! Ask yourself:

- Are these behaviors you want when you are the customer?
- Which of these behaviors are most difficult for you personally?

Many of these behaviors will be dealt with in more actionable ways later in this guide.

No matter how good you think your service is,
it's never the best it can be.
Your employees can always find ways to make it better.
NORM BRODSKY

Weekly Ideas

1

Determine the Lifetime Value of a Customer

▶ THE IDEA

You can determine the lifetime value of each of your customers using the following formula:

Amount of money spent annually $\$\underline{\hspace{1cm}} \times$ the length in years of the relationship $\underline{\hspace{1cm}} =$ the lifetime value of the customer $\$\underline{\hspace{1cm}}.$

▶ THE IDEA IN ACTION

I frequently talk about a local dry cleaning establishment that has given me extraordinary customer service. They always take my word for things. For example, if they did not get a spot out the first time and I ask them to reclean a garment, they do so immediately and graciously. They often charge me nothing for extra services such as replacing a button or sewing up a tear, and they always give me special service, remembering my name and carrying my clothes to the car.

If I spend an average of $70 a month on cleaning, my annual value to the cleaners is $840. If I live in the area for 30 years, my lifetime value to them is $25,200 ($840 × 30 years = $25,200)! You can clearly see why this organization wants to keep my business.

If they keep the long-term picture in mind, they certainly would not want to take a chance on losing a customer worth $25,000 over a $7 cleaning bill, even if they questioned my honesty in asking to have the garment recleaned or repressed at no charge. Can you think of how many times an organization has argued with you, the customer, over a small charge and as a result, they have lost your business for a lifetime?

Can you determine the lifetime value of one of *your* customers?

Annual $_____ × _____years = $_____ lifetime value.

► **TIPS FOR IMPLEMENTATION**

Always keep the long-term relationship with a customer in mind and don't allow small things to impact a lifetime of business. Certainly, I am not advocating that you "give away the store," but I am encouraging you to think in bigger terms than just the immediate request. Doing so is what builds customer loyalty.

Another reason for the importance of building customer loyalty is a statistic that says it costs at least *five times* as much to get a new customer as it does to keep an old one. So, you will help keep expenses lower and profits higher as you build customer loyalty.

2

Remember the Two Levels of Every Interaction

▶ **THE IDEA**

Every interaction we have with someone has two levels—the *Business level* of meeting their external objectives and the *Human level*, which is all about how that interaction makes them feel. Whenever you are dealing with anyone—a customer, a coworker, or an employee—make sure you have met both of these needs in your interaction, whether it is written, electronic, or face-to-face.

Human-Business Model

▶ THE IDEA IN ACTION

Because I am a professional speaker and author, I travel nearly every week. I recently had a horribly traumatic experience with a credit card while I was on the road. I was in another country and I was all alone when the incident occurred. When I finally returned home and called the credit card company, I told the customer service representative the whole terrible story, almost in tears because I was reliving it again. The very first thing she said to me after hearing the whole, horrendous story was, "What's your account number?"

What level did she go to immediately? What did that tell about how she felt about *me*, a human being with an awful story? I felt as if I'd been slapped in the face!

That whole interaction could have been a positive one if she had only acknowledged my feelings and first dealt with me on a human level BEFORE she went to the business. She might have said something like, "What a terrible experience you had! You must have been really upset. Let's see how I can help you. What's your account number?" or, "I am really sorry that happened to you. Let's get it fixed right now. What's your account number?"

Notice how in just a few extra seconds she could have met both my human and my business needs, and I would have left the interaction feeling as if someone in that big, bureaucratic organization cared about me. As it was, I cancelled that credit card because I do not want to do business with an organization where people don't care about people.

**"I'm sorry, sir, but there's a four dollar
fee for asking questions."**

► TIPS FOR IMPLEMENTATION

Always remember that people are desperate to be recognized as *human beings*. They are tired of being account numbers, government numbers, and social security numbers. As technological advances are made, it will become more and more important for customer service professionals to create a personal relationship with customers, and that can only be done on the *Human* level. Doing so doesn't take a lot of extra time, but it does take an awareness of the customer's human need and the importance of that need to be acknowledged.

Here are some ways you can focus on the customer as a human being:

- Use his or her name.
- In a face-to-face interaction, make direct eye contact.
- When encountering the customer directly, carefully observe body language. The signals being sent can tell you a great deal about how the customer is feeling.
- *Listen* to what the customer is saying about things other than the business and respond to that message so the customer knows that you are listening.
- Notice something personal about the customer and comment on that—for example, pay a compliment, ask about her work, acknowledge his children.
- Look for commonalities so that you can share something personal about yourself and your life as well. This creates a personal relationship.
- Acknowledge if a customer has returned to your place of business and, if so, thank him or her.

3

Don't Take a Customer's Anger Personally

▶ **THE IDEA**

When a customer is upset, always remember that he or she is not upset at you personally; the anger is for the situation, the company, and the helplessness he or she feels.

▶ **THE IDEA IN ACTION**

When a customer is upset, think about the human-business model:

1. When the customer is terribly upset, the Human level has taken over the interaction completely. It is almost impossible to move the customer to a business solution until you have first met his or her human need for empathy and understanding. You can do so by using listening skills, staying calm, and being sincere.

2. Remember that the customer has a life outside of his or her interaction with your company. *Every customer is a unique human being.* You cannot know what his or her whole story

is. Instead, simply try to have an awareness that there are many abused, lonely, victimized people in our world today. Keeping this in mind will help you to remember that your customer may simply be angry with the world and not at you as a person. Try to find out as much as you can about the specific situation by asking sincere and empathetic questions.

3. When the customer realizes that you truly want to help him or her and not defend the company or the world, then he or she will usually allow you to move to the business level of the transaction.

▶ TIPS FOR IMPLEMENTATION

The following quotation from Lou Holtz, the coach from Notre Dame, has made a huge difference in my life:

> *Why is it that the people who need love and*
> *understanding the most, usually deserve it the least?*
>
> LOU HOLTZ

What this thought means to me is that the angriest, rudest, most obnoxious person I meet today *needs* my love and understanding the most. He or she certainly does not *deserve* to be loved and understood; however, I can *choose* to be kind to this person rather than beating him or her up like the rest of the world does.

Keeping this thought constantly in mind raises me up a level to be able to say, "Wow! This is a hurting person. I can choose to

"I don't care if it's a nice-looking vest! It was a sport coat when I brought it in here!"

treat him or her with respect, understanding, and love. Even if this person doesn't respond positively during this interaction, I can feel good because I have made the positive choice to offer kindness and understanding even when the person didn't deserve it." If you truly apply this thought, people will finally realize that you do really care about them, and they will accept and appreciate your help.

4

Surprise Coworkers and Internal Customers with Anonymous Gifts

"Jenkins! Could I see you in my office for a moment?!"

▶ THE IDEA

A workplace that is filled with appreciation and delightful surprises will always be more productive than one that is boring, ungrateful, and routine. Surprises are even more fun when they are anonymous.

▶ THE IDEA IN ACTION

A few months ago when I went to get the mail, there was a darling little basket in my door. It was filled with several small baggies that contained some frosted cookie-cutter cookies, several brownies, some Jordan almonds, and even some herbal tea bags. There was a little poem enclosed that said:

THIS LITTLE BASKET COMES TO SAY

YOU'RE A SPECIAL FRIEND IN EVERY WAY.

PASS IT ALONG BUT DON'T GET CAUGHT.

DO IT IN SECRET AS JESUS TAUGHT.

I was delighted! I enjoyed my goodies and then refilled the basket with two chocolate coffee spoons, some small packages of gourmet coffee, several gourmet biscuits, and a little bottle of jam (I never have time to bake anymore!), and left it in another person's door who I knew needed a lift. I have never found out who gave the basket to me, but it is such fun to "wonder."

Another idea is to pay for coffee for the person behind you in the cafeteria or company store. When asked why, say, "Just because it's a nice thing to do."

▶ TIPS FOR IMPLEMENTATION

This idea can be adapted to use in your workplace to surprise and delight your coworkers and internal customers. Change the faith orientation as you choose or even rewrite the whole poem. Or simply use this as an idea generator. Many organizations also use a form of "secret pals," where each person in the department draws the name of another person and agrees to give him or her little secret surprises for a period of time. Everyone loves surprises!

The most important thing to remember is that internal customers will only treat external customers as well as they are being treated themselves. If you are having fun in your workplace with your internal customers, then you will all work harder to keep up the spirits of your external customers.

5

Remember That Everyone Sees the World Differently

▶ THE IDEA

In every situation we must constantly remember that we each see the world through our own set of experiential "glasses." The way I see it is rarely the same way you see it, and the way you see it is probably *not* the way your customer sees it.

▶ THE IDEA IN ACTION

Never assume that you know how a customer, either internal or external, views a situation. *Always ask them how they see it* and then listen for understanding. Part of serving your customers is trying your best to understand how they do see a situation and then working with that perception to create a positive outcome.

I always think of a funny story I heard concerning this concept:

Two people were having lunch at a fancy pizza restaurant. The waitress asked one of the customers if she should cut

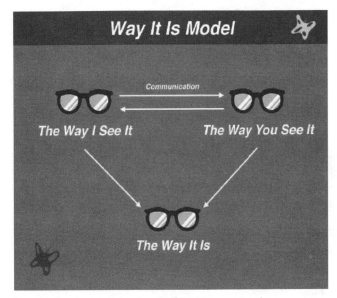

Reprinted with permission from *Building Customer Loyalty.*

his pizza in six pieces or eight. He immediately and emphatically replied, "Oh, cut it in six. I could NEVER eat eight!" His lunch partner burst into laughter.

Of course, that was the way he saw it.

▶ TIPS FOR IMPLEMENTATION

First, you must find out how a customer does see the situation, especially if you are working with a difficult customer. Tom Peters says, "Customers perceive service in their own unique, idiosyncratic, emotional, erratic, irrational, end-of-the-day, and totally human terms. Perception is all there is."

**"Sweep it up? What the heck for?
It makes great insulation!"**

The way the customer sees it is the way he or she sees it. Do not argue with that person. Just calmly paraphrase how the customer sees it, tell him or her slowly and clearly how you see it, and then ask that person for ideas for a solution or compromise so that you can both come to a "win-win." Sometimes with an internal customer, or even a family member, I actually use a copy of the "way it is model" in front of us to help maintain objectivity, pointing to the model with, "Tell me the way you see it." And then pointing again to the model when I share how "I" see it. Sometimes I even put a question mark on the part of the model that says "The way it is." Do we ever know for sure?

Whenever we can understand and accept a customer's perception of a situation, we can more easily begin to find a way to work toward a positive outcome. That does not mean that we have to *agree* with the perception but only that we respect the way the other person sees it and then use her or his help and creative thinking to come to a resolution.

6

Value Employees as "Whole" Persons

▶ **THE IDEA**

Baxter International Inc. in Chicago recently did an extensive 18-month study with their employees. They found that what an employee values most deeply is being respected as a "whole" person with a life beyond work. "The real base of [a good relationship] is the respect piece for employees and making sure it is in place, because it causes intense pain for employees when it is absent," said Alice Campbell, director of work and life programs for Baxter.

▶ **THE IDEA IN ACTION**

If you are a manager, then you know that when we ask employees to respect customers, both internal and external, it is critical that they feel respected as well. The study by Baxter International shows that they want to be respected as "whole" persons. For example, do you know the *passion* of each of your direct reports and colleagues? Do you know what they do in their free time? What makes them light up when they talk about it? If not, make

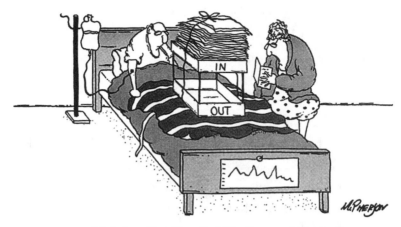

"It's from your boss. It says, 'Best wishes for a speedy recovery.'"

it a point to find out and then remember what they told you and ask them about it from time to time or bring them an article about their passion or purchase something you see that they could add to a collection. All of these examples tell them you care about them as human beings, not just workers.

I even suggest you keep a file folder on each and every person you work with. Find out special things about everybody: where they grew up, where they went to school, their spouse and children's names, what hobbies they have, where they have gone on vacation, what they have done in their lives that was exciting, what they are proud of, what their retirement dreams are.

▶ TIPS FOR IMPLEMENTATION

Here are some other creative and fun ways to respect employees as having a life beyond work:

- Ask each employee for a picture of his or her family. Single people can bring a picture of themselves with a pet, a significant other, or their extended family. Create a bulletin board or special posting place for these photographs, and be sure to include each employee's name with the picture. Make sure you keep the postings updated.

- In another part of the building have a "Good News" bulletin board where employees can share vacation and wedding pictures as well as special things that have happened to family members. Rotate these contributions every two or three weeks so that employees and managers will be inspired and eager to check the board periodically.

- Plan activities that involve employees' families such as "bring your son [or daughter, or parent, or dog] to work" days or fun fairs with booths to describe what a parent / grandparent / spouse does all day.

- When you reward an employee for extraordinary service, send the award to his or her home or invite that person's family to the celebration so that they will feel a part of it. I guarantee that they will be more helpful and understanding in the future when that employee puts in extra time at the office!

- Create T-shirts for employees' children or grandchildren that say, "My Mom/Dad/Grandpa/Grandma works at _____." This will not only delight them, but it is free marketing!

Do these things in as classy a way as you can afford so that employees feel valued and respected. It is especially important that managers spend time learning about their individual employees—family situations and names, hobbies, and special interests. As employees feel valued as "whole" persons, they will be better able to create relationships with customers.

*If you just treat your customers with warmth
and love and respect, you'll have so much money
that you won't know what to do with it. . . .
People want to be treated like kings all the time.
It's so easy.*

JOHN TSCHOL,
SERVICE QUALITY INSTITUTE

7

Listen with Your Heart

► **THE IDEA**

The Chinese characters that make up the verb "to listen" tell us something significant about this important customer-service skill.

The Chinese characters which make up the verb "to listen"

Ear

You

Eyes

Undivided Attention

Heart

The Transit Authority makes a desperate attempt to promote a friendlier atmosphere by hiring hospitality hostesses.

▶ THE IDEA IN ACTION

Remember the human-business model and the idea that every customer (and coworker and employee) is a unique human being? My brother, who is a consultant in Thailand, sent me this Chinese symbol, and it has meant a great deal to me in my work with customer service.

On the left-hand side, the ear is represented—listening with our ears and our head and our intellect, listening for the facts or the *Business* level of the transaction. Unfortunately, many managers and customer service professionals stop at this point. But on the right-hand side we see the true meaning of "listening":

- Listening from our own personhood—one human being listening to another, bringing our own life learnings and experiences to the encounter
- Listening with our eyes for body language (especially on the telephone we must sharpen our skills to listen for tone of voice and emotion, since we cannot "see" the customer)
- Listening with our undivided attention—focusing completely on that customer and his or her situation
- Listening with our hearts—empathy, the cornerstone of listening. I love this definition of empathy: "Empathy is your pain in my heart."

▶ **TIPS FOR IMPLEMENTATION**

Write on a 3 × 5 card the following reminder: "Am I listening with my heart?" and post it somewhere in your work area where you will see it every day. Some people even keep some form of a heart in their workspace as a constant reminder. When we are truly listening with our hearts, we are focused on human beings and building relationships of service.

8

Reframe How You View Mis-Takes in Your Organization

PART ONE

▶ **THE IDEA**

Have you ever had a manager yell at you and embarrass you in front of a coworker? If you are a manager, how do you react when one of your employees makes a mistake? I have seen managers who yell, lecture, punish, threaten, and humiliate. After many years of working in customer service, I truly believe that most employees are trying to do their best, and they do not make mistakes on purpose. Also, I have come to believe that as long as we have human beings working for us, mistakes will occur.

Therefore, I want to suggest a way for you to "reframe" the concept of a mistake. Most of us think of a "mistake" as "bad" or a "failure." However, because we are all human beings, there *will* be mistakes in our organizations. The question becomes not "Will

**"He drank the last cup of coffee and
didn't make a fresh pot."**

there be any mistakes?" but rather "When a mistake is made, how will we handle it?"

I ask people in my training sessions to hyphenate the word "mistake" and to think of it as a "Mis-Take." Doesn't that have a different feeling? I think of the movies where it may take hundreds of "takes" to get a final print. Therefore, a "Mis-Take" is not bad or a failure but rather just one thing that didn't work.

REFRAME:

A "Mis-Take" becomes an opportunity to learn.

▶ THE IDEA IN ACTION

Most of us, if we are completely honest, would like to hide our mistakes; however, if they are viewed as "Mis-Takes," then everyone can be comfortable to share theirs and all can learn from them. I even suggest to organizations that they have a "Mis-Take" of the week and have fun with whoever has made the biggest one. You might even have a traveling trophy of some kind that the "winner" keeps on his or her desk for a week!

An employee at one company I consult with told me about how they handle "Mis-Takes" in their office. The person who accumulates the most "voids" on a particular day gets a crown and the title of "Void King or Queen for the Day." They have chosen to have fun with what naturally will happen in their very stressful jobs.

▶ TIPS FOR IMPLEMENTATION

Not only does this opportunity create a wonderful sharing and learning atmosphere, but it also gives you permission to admit your "Mis-Takes" and to fix them rather then pretending they didn't happen until an angry customer lets someone know. In fact, a "Mis-Take," if fixed quickly and in a creative way, can become a wonderful opportunity to create a delighted customer and ultimately make you, the employee, feel even more valuable!

9

Reframe How You View Mis-Takes in Your Organization

PART TWO

▶ **THE IDEA**

REFRAME:

A "Mis-Take" becomes an opportunity to create
a loyal customer.

▶ **THE IDEA IN ACTION**

Study after study has shown that one of the four things all our customers want is *Recovery* when the organization has made a "Mis-Take." They want us to apologize sincerely, fix it, and then do something extra. With creative thinking, we can dazzle customers by surprising and delighting them with the way we handle a "Mis-Take," and therefore, we build customer loyalty and provide our customers with a wonderful story to tell and retell their friends!

"Sorry about the mix-up, Mr. Bixford. We'll be moving you to a semi-private room shortly."

Recently, I ordered several items from a catalog. When I received the order, I discovered that I had been charged twice for a pair of silk pants. The employee had inadvertently punched in the number "2," which had automatically doubled the price. When I called the company to report the error, the customer service rep was wonderful. He not only used some humor ("Why would anyone want *two* pair of orange silk pants anyway?"), but he also apologized sincerely, immediately fixed the problem, and then, to create a loyal customer, he shared with me that he had deducted all charges for postage as an apology for their "Mis-Take." Since it was a big order, that amount was substantial, so I was delighted and will continue to order from them and recommend them to others even though they did goof up!

It may be difficult for some managers to lighten up enough to reframe a negative into a positive in this way; however, I have found that in organizations where employees are allowed to make "Mis-Takes" and are encouraged to share them, ultimately the number of "Mis-Takes" decreases because employees are functioning in an atmosphere of support and trust rather than fear.

▶ TIPS FOR IMPLEMENTATION

We live in the "Age of Empowerment," and while many informed managers are giving their employees *permission* to be empowered, many of them are not giving the employees *protection* when they make a "Mis-Take." If you give your employees both permission *and* protection, you will have employees who feel respected and valued, and that will translate to your customers' satisfaction and to your bottom line.

As an employee, remember that supervisors and managers make "Mis-Takes," too, so be forgiving and learn just as they expect you to do!

10

Decorate Your Cubicle or Workspace with Things That Remind You of Giving Good Service

▶ THE IDEA

I have a master's degree in Adult Continuing Education. One of the things we know about adult learning is that we need "anchors," or things to remind us of ideas and concepts we have learned. When you discover an idea in this guide that really excites you, create something to put up in your cubicle as a reminder to use the idea in your very important work.

▶ THE IDEA IN ACTION

- I happen to love quotations, so I decorate my workspace and every area of my home with quotations I love. Four that I have everywhere are:

*Be kind and merciful. Let no one ever come to you
without coming away better and happier.*
MOTHER TERESA

*Why is it that the people who need love and
understanding the most usually deserve it the least?*
LOU HOLTZ

Be kind. Everyone you meet is carrying something.
ANONYMOUS

*Never believe that a few caring people can't change
the world. For indeed, that's all who ever have.*
MARGARET MEADE

- Many companies have inspirational posters you can pur-chase as reminders, or you can make your own with colored markers. You might also create a collage of pictures cut from magazines that remind you of good service.
- Some organizations give telephone employees a heart-shaped mirror with the reminder, "You can *hear* a smile!"
- Kaiser Permanente in Santa Clara, California, gives employees a lovely silver mirror with stars on it that says, "Say it with a smile!"
- If you often talk to the same customers, internal or external, ask for a picture of them and create a "great customers" bul-letin board.
- Consider having a "Decorate your Cube for Service Day" and give a prize to the one whose workspace most creatively exemplifies a service culture.

▶ TIPS FOR IMPLEMENTATION

A work area that contains constant motivational reminders of good service will not only create a more empathetic, productive atmosphere for you, but it will also encourage others around you and get their creative juices going!

11

Celebrate the Gift of Life!

▶ **THE IDEA**

I love the following poem:

YESTERDAY IS HISTORY.

TOMORROW IS A MYSTERY.

TODAY IS A GIFT.

THAT'S WHY WE CALL IT "THE PRESENT"!

▶ **THE IDEA IN ACTION**

When I speak to an audience, I sometimes share this beautiful thought with them. Because I often speak about one of my previous books, *CARE Packages for the Workplace: Dozens of Little Things You Can Do to Regenerate Spirit at Work*, the idea of each day being a gift is central to my message: we each can choose to send metaphorical CARE packages, to make a difference in every interaction we have with anyone. Every day offers us unlimited opportunities to make a difference in our world by showing just a little more CARE-ing to those around us.

I also share with them my strong belief that every person we meet is a gift to us. We have the choice of either "unwrapping" that gift, making a human-level connection by finding out something about that very special person, or discarding the gift, choosing to take care of just the business at hand and simply ignoring the human being in front of us. In our world today I see so many unwrapped gifts—lonely, hurting people about whom no one seems to care.

Sometimes we only have time to untie the ribbon. Other times we can take a short peek inside that gift by asking some personal questions. If we are lucky, we might have time to dig down deep inside that package and find the treasure that is hidden there by learning someone's unique story.

I have made it my personal mission in life to try my hardest to recognize people as *human beings with a story* and to acknowledge their uniqueness in whatever ways time will allow. Sometimes it is only a quick smile or touch on the arm, a "thank you" for going out of their way for me, or a simple personal question and then truly listening to the answer. At other times I am blessed to be able to really hear some of that person's story, and then I always feel as if I have made a new and special friend.

Several years ago, I walked into the women's restroom at O'Hare Airport. I noticed a woman inside who was cleaning. She was all hunched over, listlessly going through the motions of her job. I walked up to her, touched her on the arm, looked her

"It certainly is an enthusiastic staff."

right in the eyes, and said, "Thank you so much for keeping this washroom clean. You're really making a difference for all of us who travel."

She perked up, started cleaning with a passion, and by the time I left, she was handing towels out to all the women who were washing their hands. I left with tears in my eyes, for that cost me nothing. However, in that one statement I was able to give that precious woman a CARE package, telling her that she was of value—*and* I left with a full heart and the joy of being alive.

▶ TIPS FOR IMPLEMENTATION

Consider keeping a "Blessings Journal," where at the end of each day you write the special things that have happened that day. Even on the darkest days, try to find one or two things that have touched you in some way.

Mother Teresa said, "Be kind and merciful. Let no one ever come to you without coming away better and happier." May I challenge you to make that your philosophy of life? Every day *is* a gift, and no matter what your work is, you have the opportunity every day to open the gifts all around you. Don't let the tyranny of the urgent rob you of the very special gift of CARE-ing!

12

Remember the Concept of the Emotional Bank Account

PART ONE

▶ **THE IDEA**

Refill others' emotional bank accounts. Stephen Covey, the author of *The 7 Habits of Highly Effective People* (Free Press) talks about the concept of the emotional bank account. Each day in your work you get deposits and withdrawals. Which do you get the most of in your job? Think about what happens when you get withdrawal after withdrawal. You are overdrawn!

Your customers and coworkers also get deposits and withdrawals. When an overdrawn customer interacts with an overdrawn customer service person, the interaction will probably not be positive! Therefore, it is important to help your team members keep their emotional bank accounts refilled.

▶ THE IDEA IN ACTION

Can you tell when a team member is overdrawn? Then, **give him or her a deposit**. Get your creative juices going to think up as many ways of giving deposits as you can. Here are a few you might use:

- Give them a pat on the back, a big smile, or even a hug.
- Take them to lunch.
- Offer to help them.
- Draw a funny picture or write a poem and leave it on their desk.
- Ask if they want to talk.
- Invite them for a walk around the building.
- Ask about their family.
- Bring them a treat.

When customers are overdrawn, here are some things you might do to help refill their emotional bank accounts:

- Really listen and be empathetic.
- Ask them about their family.
- Do something extra for them.
- Tell them something funny.
- Ask for their feedback or advice.
- Make them feel they are the most important person in the world to you at that moment.

▶ TIPS FOR IMPLEMENTATION

One teleservices company with whom I've worked had a great idea. Over one hundred customer service reps had cubicles in a huge room in their building. They made several placards that they mounted on sticks which read, **"I NEED A DEPOSIT!"** Whenever they had a really bad call and their emotional bank account was overdrawn, they simply held up the placard over their cubicle and the folks who weren't on a call came over to cheer them up and make a deposit!

Always remember: when you refill someone else's emotional bank account, you are also getting a deposit in your own.

I don't know what your destiny will be,
but one thing I know:
the only ones among you who will be really happy
are those who have sought
and found how to serve.

ALBERT SCHWEITZER

13

Remember the Concept of the Emotional Bank Account

PART TWO

▶ THE IDEA

Refill your own emotional bank account. Can you tell when your own emotional bank account is getting overdrawn? Sometimes a bad day begins at home when your alarm doesn't go off, your toast gets burned, you have a bad hair day, you miss the train, and you arrive at work to find the boss is planning on monitoring you. Then you have one difficult customer after another.

If you don't get your emotional bank account refilled, you may end up arguing with a customer or a coworker and creating a negative interaction. Becoming aware that your account is getting low and then doing something about it will help you to continue to create positive interactions even when things do go wrong.

It dawned on Carol that today was the day the
realtor had said he wanted to show the house.

▶ THE IDEA IN ACTION

Make a list of things that bring you joy or that you like to do. Here
are some of the things on my list:

- Go shopping!
- Talk to a friend.
- Count my blessings.

- Take five-minute "vacations"—either a walk around the building or perhaps just go to the ladies' room, shut the door, and go to the Bahamas for five minutes. (I can do anything I want and it doesn't cost any money!)
- Ask for help.
- Buy myself a bag of potato chips.
- Play the piano.
- Take a hot bubble bath.
- Have a cup of tea.
- Call someone who loves me.
- Read a good book.
- Do something positive for someone else.
- Pray.
- Focus on someone I love.

Of course, I can't do some of these at work, but the key is to recognize that I'm overdrawn and then consciously do something that will give me a deposit.

▶ TIPS FOR IMPLEMENTATION

I have a brother who lived in Singapore, and several years ago for Christmas he gave me a Chinese gift—a little leather ball (almost like a hackey-sack) on a long bamboo stick. When I called to thank him and ask what it was for, he answered, "You keep that right by your desk and when you're having a bad day or you've done something great and no one has noticed, just take it and give yourself a little pat on the back." And, I *do*! You can make yourself a ball on a stick, too, and give yourself those pats when you need them!

14

Decorate Hallways and Walls with Inspirational Quotations and Graphics

► THE IDEA

What do your hallways look like? Most buildings I visit are pretty dismal beyond the reception area. Tom Peters says that if your hallways are boring, chances are that everything you do in your organization is boring!

Have a poster party. Bring several flip chart pads, lots of colored markers, and invite anyone who wants to come to bring some of their favorite thoughts and quotations.

► THE IDEA IN ACTION

Whenever I speak to an audience, whether it is 30 or 3,000, I line the walls of the room or ballroom with 50 to 100 brightly colored, laminated flip charts with quotations and graphics. I want to create an atmosphere of inspiration, stimulation, and fun. Here are a few flip charts my daughter Erin has drawn that you may copy:

"Praise is like sunlight to the human spirit: We cannot flower and grow without it."

Jess Fair

"There are two ways of spreading light: to be the candle...

or the mirror that reflects it."

Edith Wharton

Reprinted with permission from *The Creative Commumicator*.

▶ TIPS FOR IMPLEMENTATION

You may decide to have the charts laminated so they will last longer. You can have this done for about $3.75 per chart. Other organizations have installed large clear plastic frames, and they rotate the posters periodically throughout the building. You will be amazed at the artistic talent people in your organization have that you knew nothing about, and the change in atmosphere will ultimately impact productivity and creativity in your workplace. If people feel that they are working in a happy place, they will make those around them happier!

> *Be it furniture, clothes, or health care,*
> *many industries today are marketing*
> *nothing more than commodities—*
> *no more, no less.*
> *What will make the difference in the long run*
> *is the care and feeding of customers.*
>
> –MICHAEL AND TIMOTHY MESCON

15

Hold Focus Groups

PART ONE

► **THE IDEA**

Hold *customer* focus groups at least once per quarter. Since customers' needs are constantly changing, it is important to listen to them to find out what they really want and how you're doing in serving them. It also helps to build loyalty when you ask a customer to participate in a focus group because you are showing how much you value his or her opinion. So, it is a win-win situation for everyone!

► **THE IDEA IN ACTION**

You can get excellent feedback from customers in a focus group when you ask three questions:

1. On a scale of 1 to 10, with 1 being "horrible" and 10 being "extraordinary," how did we do the last time you had an interaction with us? This will give you a quantitative score you can use as an ongoing comparison.

2. What did we do well? This gives you positive information in an open-ended question.

3. What could we have done better? This open-ended question will give you valuable information about where service is breaking down, and if a "Mis-take" was made, you have an opportunity to recover.

Due to recent cutbacks, several major airlines have eliminated their snack carts.

► **TIPS FOR IMPLEMENTATION**

These same questions may also be used on a weekly basis by every employee. If each employee called one customer a week at random, can you imagine the valuable information you would receive, the feeling of being "in on things" for each employee, and the loyal customers you would create? The whole process only takes two to three minutes.

16

Hold Focus Groups

PART TWO

► **THE IDEA**

Hold *employee* focus groups at least once per quarter. Employees also need to be heard. Not only do they have the best ideas because they are closest to the customers, but they also need to feel valued and respected by the organization. One of the best ways to do so is to hold short focus groups on a regular basis. When employees feel the organization is listening to their concerns and ideas, they will become more loyal and will do an even better job of serving their customers.

► **THE IDEA IN ACTION**

The ideal employee focus group is made up of about six to seven people. It is usually best to keep frontline folks together, supervisors together, managers, and senior managers each in their own group. Concerns and ideas will be very different for each group, and employees usually do not speak freely in front of their superiors.

"Unfortunately, ma'am, this airplane is not equipped with rest rooms. We do, however, have this personal lavatory and a privacy blanket for your convenience."

Several things are critical if these focus groups are to be perceived as important:

1. Everyone must have a chance to attend one focus group at least once a year, if they choose.
2. The facilitators of these groups must be specially trained.

(I have even developed a certification process for focus group facilitation to ensure consistency and quality.)

3. The information must go directly and immediately to senior management, and they must be held accountable to make changes and then to notify employees regularly of the results of their input.

▶ **TIPS FOR IMPLEMENTATION**

Each focus group should last from 25 to 30 minutes and should be very positively focused so that it doesn't become a gripe session. I begin each group with some posted guidelines, and then I ask two questions:

1. What do you love about working here?
2. What are some of your concerns about where things aren't working well, and what are your ideas for solutions?

I then write the participants' *exact words* on the flip chart, always beginning with the positive and focusing the concerns on creative solutions. I am always amazed at the valuable information and creative ideas that come from these groups! Employees know exactly where service, both internal and external, is breaking down, and they have wonderful ideas to fix things. Management only needs to ask and then listen.

17

Give Yourself a Hand!

▶ **THE IDEA**

Whenever you have done something special such as turned an angry customer around, solved a difficult problem, or made a sale, celebrate your success. Give yourself a hand!

▶ **THE IDEA IN ACTION**

Here are some delightful ways to show appreciation for yourself:

- Remember how in grade school you often traced around your hand? Do that again, and this time post it on the wall near your desk. When you have done something great and no one has noticed, just back up to it and "Give yourself a hand!" I guarantee it will make you feel better.
- After I had spoken to the Department of State in Michigan, I received a call from an employee at one of the driver's license facilities. She said that soon after I'd been there, she lost one of her best leather gloves, and she was really upset with herself. However, as she began thinking about my training, she had a brainstorm. She decided to take the

lemons and make lemonade—she took the one remaining glove, stuffed it with panty hose, sewed little bows on it, and mounted it on a stick. She took it to work, and she said that now the *customers* even ask for a "pat on the back!"

• A participant in one of my sessions sent me a rubber hand on a flat plastic stick. Another client sent me three little plastic hands on one handle. When you shake it, the hands make a clapping sound. Whenever someone makes a sale or opens a new account in their office, everyone gives them a hand.

▶ TIPS FOR IMPLEMENTATION

According to one recent study, 65 percent of American workers said they received *no* appreciation for all the good work they did last year. Even if you do not receive appreciation from your super-

"There you go, sir."

visor or manager, you can still appreciate yourself! It is a positive choice you can make. We all need our emotional bank accounts refilled, and these are some fun ways to refill your own account without waiting for someone else to do it. You can also use them to congratulate others in your workplace because everyone needs to be appreciated.

The only way to know how customers see your business is to look at it through their eyes.

DANIEL R. SCOGGIN,
PRESIDENT AND CEO,
TGI FRIDAY'S, INC.

18

Five Loyalty Builders

▶ **THE IDEA**

Every day in your job try to build relationships with your customers so that they will be loyal to your organization. Loyal customers keep your organization in business which, in turn, assures the need for jobs like yours. Research has shown that there are five loyalty builders. Challenge yourself to use each of these loyalty builders at least once a day.

▶ **THE IDEA IN ACTION**

Here are five customer loyalty builders:

1. Trusting the customer
2. Going the extra mile for the customer
3. Recovering when a "Mis-Take" is made
4. Appreciating the customer
5. Taking initiative to help the customer

"I'll be going to the Bahamas for a week starting tomorrow. This should tide you over 'til I get back."

▶ TIPS FOR IMPLEMENTATION

Notice that *caring* is the most important underlying component of each loyalty builder. When Cambridge Reports did a study on customer satisfaction for electric utilities, sponsored by the Edison Electrical Institute, they found that the single most important factor mentioned was caring. This research has been replicated over and over.

With your work team, discuss each of these loyalty builders and determine:

1. *What you are already doing* in each of the areas listed above.
2. *What you need to do* in the future to ensure your connection to your customers.
3. *Brainstorm specific actions you can begin to implement in each area* to create even greater customer loyalty for your organization.

As you think about meeting the human needs of your customers as well as their business needs, and as you practice these five loyalty builders every day, they will become a part of the way *you* do your job, and you will be a successful customer service professional!

19

Celebrate Small Wins

▶ **THE IDEA**

Sometimes organizations and individuals think that unless something major is accomplished, they do not have the "right" to cele-

After the team lost 20 consecutive games, Coach Farnsworth
did his best to help his players regain their confidence.

brate. If we wait for huge achievements, sometimes we are waiting forever, it seems, so I suggest that you celebrate small wins and accomplishments and celebrate often. Creating an atmosphere of appreciation and celebration is one of the keys to a productive workplace.

► THE IDEA IN ACTION

- Stiles Machinery in Grand Rapids, Michigan, has a large bell on a frame that is their celebration tool. Whenever anyone makes a big sale, they ring the bell on the intercom so that the whole company can know and cheer them on.

- The Humor Project in Saratoga Springs, New York, has a wonderful product catalog of items to make your workplace more fun. One of my favorites is a set of plastic hands on a handle that clap when you shake the handle. These are great fun to "applaud" work well done. (You can order the catalog from 800-600-4242.)

- Some organizations use the intercom or e-mail to share congratulatory messages with everyone. One company plays a piece of energetic music when a sale is made, while another turns on a siren.

- You might bring treats for everyone when a small goal is reached or let everyone have an extra 30 minutes at lunch.

- Do a quarterly video of the progress your department has made, and let the employees be the stars.

▶ TIPS FOR IMPLEMENTATION

Get your creative juices going to think of ways you can celebrate small wins in your department. You can even get your customers involved in the celebration. Ask them to share in the treats or give an employee "a hand" or vote for their favorite employee. They will have fun cheering you on!

Brainstorm Ways You Can Enhance Your Customer's Experience

PART ONE

▶ **THE IDEA**

One of the ways to build customer loyalty is to do things that surprise and delight your customers. A technique to find ways to do this is to hold a brainstorming session to come up with creative ideas that will enhance the customer's experience and make your job more fun.

▶ **THE IDEA IN ACTION**

Learn the technique of brainstorming.

One of the best techniques for brainstorming is to start with a silly example to get people thinking "out of the box." I have people get into teams of five or six (don't have any more than this number, or not everyone will participate), and we go over the rules of brainstorming:

- No criticizing.
- Encourage free-wheeling discussion.
- Encourage the combination and improvement of ideas.
- Don't discuss or evaluate the ideas while generating the list.
- It's okay to piggyback on others' ideas.
- Quantity, not quality, of ideas is important.

Then this is their "assignment":

Each of your groups owns a Laundromat. At the end of the year you are left with 3689 unmatched socks. I will give you three minutes to see which team can brainstorm the most wild and crazy ideas of things you can do with all those socks!

We then see which team came up with the most ideas and have each team share their favorite ideas. Some of the craziest ideas have been to use them as doggy earmuffs, coffee filters, weapons (filled with rocks) and Beanie Baby sleeping bags! What makes this exercise fun is getting people loosened up in their thinking and having fun with something that is out of the ordinary. Then, I ask them to keep this same creative spirit to brainstorm something related to their work, such as ways to appreciate their customers.

▶ TIPS FOR IMPLEMENTATION

You can choose any sort of fun situation to learn the technique of brainstorming, such as all the uses you can imagine for a paper clip.

"We apologize if we startled you, folks. However,
state law requires that we perform unannounced
Heimlich maneuver drills once every month."

The important thing is to get everyone thinking "out of the box."
You will have fun, and after the first 10 or 12 ideas, the group will
really begin to be creative. Give them enough time to get loosened
up but usually no more than five minutes so that everyone is kept
fully involved. You can also try the process by yourself; however,
you will find that you are stimulated by others and their ideas.

21

Brainstorm Ways You Can Enhance Your Customer's Experience

Part Two

► **THE IDEA**

A Moment of Truth is a *memory* for the customer, so one of the best ways we can create customer loyalty is to make that experience a positive, memorable one for the customer who will leave thinking, "Wow! That was really special!" Enhancers are the little extra things you can do in a typical service moment to make it positively memorable. Enhancers can *create* memories. Positive memories over time create loyalty.

► **THE IDEA IN ACTION**

Here are some enhancers that others have added to create extraordinary experiences for their customers:

- A cleaning establishment keeps its customer records on computer. When the computer shows that the customer has spent a total of $500 with that cleaner, the order they are picking up is free. This unexpected surprise has dazzled their customers.
- At the Ritz-Carlton hotel, employees *escort* guests rather then simply pointing them someplace in the hotel.
- A suburban Illinois bank serves coffee and donut holes at all times in its lobby. They also have a play area for customers' children and provide childcare while the customer is doing business.
- An auto parts store loans its customers videotapes they have created that explain how to do various car repairs.
- A pediatric dentist provides telephones in his reception area with the number of the tooth fairy posted beside them. The children who are his customers may call the tooth fairy (a bedridden person in a local rest home) whenever they visit his office.
- A speaker ends her presentations by giving each audience member a "Pass It On" card that says, "The world is more special because you're in it!"
- A bank teller keeps a pad of Post-it notes in her drawer that say, "I'm glad I saw you today." While she is transacting the customer's business, she signs one of the notes and slips it (unknown to the customer) into the customer's bankbook or other paper from the transaction.
- At a restaurant when the waiter or waitress brings the check, he or she also brings two small complimentary glasses of dessert sherry as a thank you for dining with them.

- The Savings Bank of Rockville, Connecticut, gave customers a foldover business card with the bank logo on the front. On the inside it says, "Who says The Savings Bank of Rockville Doesn't Give Away Free Samples?" A dime is pasted to the underside of the card.

- A retail store clerk enhances each customer's experience by suggesting accessories for what they have purchased. The store clerk will often even take time to go to another floor to bring back matching items to share with the customer.

- A car dealer hires a retired gentleman to serve coffee to people waiting in line in their cars for automotive service early in the morning.

- A salesperson in a large retail store took time to write a thank-you note for my purchase at her store. She even remembered a trip I mentioned I'd be taking and commented on that in her note.

- A jewelry store keeps a record of the dates of anniversaries and wives' or girlfriends' birthdays. Then 30 days before the date, they send a card to the husband or boyfriend at his place of work reminding him of the occasion.

- Nordstrom in Oak Brook, Illinois, lists its closing time as 9:00 p.m. However, they often stay open later to accommodate a customer.

- A production worker keeps a supply of stickers that say, "This product was created with care by _____." He writes in his name and attaches it to the product.

- An amusement park places video monitors that play cartoons and other specials for the customers to watch while they are waiting in line.

- A customer service rep always has a bowl of seasonal candy on her desk for her customers to enjoy.
- A sales representative I know keeps a bulletin board in his office. On it he displays pictures of his customers' children and families.
- Gateway Cleaners has a customer bulletin board where they display stories about their customers as well as pictures of new homes, new babies, and trips their customers have taken.
- USAA insurance declared a 25 percent rebate on auto insurance for everyone who served in the Desert Storm combat area during hostilities. They also set up a hotline, the Desert Storm Assistance Center, so that should a member be killed, the survivors could call in and the company would then take care of everything—life insurance, bank account, investment management, property insurance— with one phone call.
- American Airlines has authorized their flight attendants to issue cleaning vouchers right on the plane whenever they accidentally spill on the customer.
- When a friend of mine was training in another city, a waiter in the hotel where she was staying overheard her say it was her birthday that week. On the evening of her special day, he brought a piece of cake with a sparkler on the top to her room.

"Granted, it doesn't have the versatility
of our other models, but most people
find it much easier to play."

► TIPS FOR IMPLEMENTATION

Let these examples be idea generators. Begin to think about enhancers that you like as a customer and how they help build your loyalty.

22

Brainstorm Ways You Can Enhance Your Customer's Experience

PART THREE

▶ **THE IDEA**

Apply the idea of enhancers to your *own* very important job. What can you do at key moments of truth with your customers to surprise them and enhance their experience? Be as creative as you can be with this exercise. Get "out of the box" and don't fall into thinking "this is the way it's always been" or "this is what we do in our industry." The best ideas are often the most outrageous ones or those that are the most fun. For example, a person who works in a Honda dealership I recently worked with bakes chocolate chip cookies each day and serves them to the people who come into his showroom. He told me he purposely burns the first batch just a bit in order to get that special aroma in the building! Remember the idea is to surprise and delight *your* customer.

"And how about you, ma'am? Would you like
some ground pepper on your salad?"

► THE IDEA IN ACTION

Creative enhancers: The purpose of this brainstorming exercise is to get *quantity*, not quality, by listing as many ways as you can think of to enhance your customer's experience. Keep going until you have at least 20 ideas of ways you can delight your customers, because the best ones usually come later in your creative process. This is also a fun exercise to do with several of your coworkers.

1. _____

_____

2. _____

_____

3. _____

_____

4. _____

_____

5. _____

_____

6. _____

_____

7. _____

_____

8. _____

_____

9. _____

_____

10. _____

_____

11. _____

_____

12. _____

_____

13. _____

_____

14. _____

15. _____

16. _____

17. _____

18. _____

19. _____

20. _____

What was the *worst* idea you came up with?

_____

_____

_____

_____

Now think of two *good* things about that idea.

1. _____

2. _____

What was the *best* idea you came up with?

_____

_____

_____

_____

Choose at least one of your ideas to implement immediately in your work.

▶ TIPS FOR IMPLEMENTATION

Wonderful, creative, exciting ideas come from this exercise. I suggest that you take your list of ideas and prioritize them according to whether they are (1) immediately actionable, (2) need a little time, or (3) need more research or even policy changes before implementation. Then choose one idea a quarter to implement to surprise and delight your customers. If you do this as a team, not only will you have several years' worth of good ideas, but this is also a form of continuous improvement and adds excitement to your job and surprises and delights your customers.

23

Focus on What You <u>Can</u> Do

▶ **THE IDEA**

After eleven years of working in customer service training, I have come to the belief that about 80 percent of good customer service is creative thinking—not simply focusing on the specific thing the customer asks for but always thinking of options and alternatives that may be even better for that customer.

▶ **THE IDEA IN ACTION**

The key to great customer service is to focus on what you *can* do, not on what you *can't* do!

When I wanted a certain dress at a retail store that they did not have in my size, a salesperson called eighteen stores in nine different states to try to find it for me. When she couldn't find the exact dress I wanted, she apologized with lots of empathy, saying "I know how much you wanted that dress, and I tried my very best to find it for you. I called eighteen stores in nine different states, and no one had that dress in your size. I am so very sorry I could

not find the dress you wanted so badly." However, then she offered me an option. She said she had found a dress of the same color with similar styling and if I wanted to try it, she would send it out at no charge. Even though I didn't get the exact thing I wanted, I still felt loyal to this store because the salesperson really tried to meet my need and didn't stop with just one or two tries.

▶ TIPS FOR IMPLEMENTATION

The important thing here is to get your creative juices going so you don't simply stop at the customer's expressed business need. Sometimes you know about alternatives that the customer doesn't, and you may be able to offer something even better than the customer requested. The bottom line, however, is that even if after all your creative thinking, you cannot meet the customer's *business* need, you can always meet the customer's *human* need for empathy, caring, and giving it your best try. Although the customer may not be happy, he or she will respect that you really tried and that you cared, and *that* will keep the customer coming back!

Expectations are critical when you serve customers.
Meet them to satisfy the customer.
Exceed them to make the customer love you.

ROBERT A. PETERSON

24

Have Fun with Stories

▶ THE IDEA

The pastor of a church in Houston, Texas, for many years had a very creative ministry. "The Matter of Fax" was distributed weekly to about 350 people, including then-President Clinton and then-Governor Bush. Included in the distribution list were pastors, politicians, business owners, individuals, media outlets, and missionaries. He faxed weekly messages of inspiration, hope, and cheer to anyone who wanted to be included. You can have fun in your organizations by sharing stories that you have enjoyed, especially stories of great customer service.

▶ THE IDEA IN ACTION

This is one of the stories the pastor sent me:

> A little bird was flying south for the winter. It got so cold it froze up and fell to the ground in a large field. While it was lying there, a cow came by and dropped some manure

on it. As it lay there in the pile of manure, it began to realize how warm it was. The manure was actually thawing
him out! He lay there all warm and happy, and soon began
to sing for joy. A passing cat heard the little bird singing
and came to investigate. Following the sound, the cat discovered the bird under the pile of manure and promptly
dug him out—and then ate him!

The morals of the story are:
1. Not everyone who drops manure on you is your
   enemy.
2. Not everyone who digs you out of a pile of
   manure is your friend.
3. When you are in the manure, keep your mouth
   shut!

He ended by saying, "Well, I will take my chances singing
anytime!"

► TIPS FOR IMPLEMENTATION

There are many resources for stories available—daily newspapers,
magazines such as *Guideposts*, compilations such as the *Chicken
Soup for the Soul* books, and your own true life stories. Today there
are many sources on the Internet for inspirational stories.
Although it is important not to send out unwanted spam, sharing
something inspirational with your team can help to raise morale
and encourage good service. People remember stories, and they
often teach lessons more powerfully than any training course!

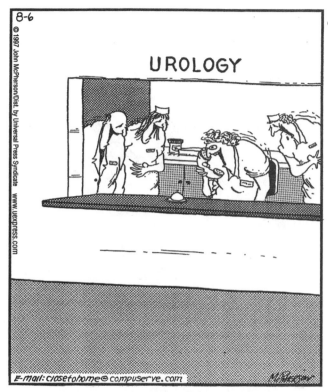

"Urology department. Can you hold?"

25

You Don't Learn Anything with Your Mouth Open

▶ THE IDEA

One of the best ways to persuade others is to listen to them. Remember that we have two ears and only one mouth for a reason!

▶ THE IDEA IN ACTION

Important Rules for Good Listening:

1. Remember—it is impossible to listen and talk at the same time.
2. Make direct eye contact with the person if you are face-to-face; find a way to focus on the individual human being if you are on the telephone.
3. Listen for the main ideas.
4. Fight off distractions.
5. React to the message, not to the person.

6. Ask questions.
7. Don't think of what you want to say next while the other person is talking.
8. Take notes, if necessary.
9. Treat the other person as if he or she were the most important person on earth.
10. Focus on the other person, not on you!

Bob Swilnard was a lifeguard with an attitude.

▶ TIPS FOR IMPLEMENTATION

Talk is cheap because supply exceeds demand. Do not miss the many valuable opportunities to hold your tongue and listen to what the other person is saying. Talk less. Learn to listen. Your ears will never get you into trouble. I recently heard a person say, "You can tell how good a parent / spouse / (I would add "customer service person") you are by the number of bite marks on your tongue!"

26

Beautiful People Don't Just Happen

▶ THE IDEA

As a professional speaker, every month I send the people on my database an e-mail newsletter (you can subscribe to it at www .barbaraglanz.com), and in each edition I share "Quotes of the Month"—thoughts that have touched my heart in special ways. This is the thought I used in a recent newsletter:

> *The most beautiful people we have known are those*
> *who have known defeat, known suffering,*
> *known struggle, known loss, and have found their*
> *way out of the depths. These persons have an appreciation,*
> *a sensitivity, and an understanding of life that*
> *fills them with compassion, gentleness,*
> *and a deep loving concern.*
> *Beautiful people do not just happen.*
>
> ELISABETH KÜBLER-ROSS

To help customers fit into the bathing suits they wanted, Felman's Department Store wisely installed stair-stepping machines in its women's department.

► THE IDEA IN ACTION

As a young person, my whole life seemed to fit the plans that I had for myself and my future. Certainly I had my share of disappointment and hurt; however, I was always able to get back on track and meet all the goals I had set for myself. Then, at age 29 my whole life fell apart in tragedies that were completely beyond my control!

Chronologically, in 18 months, my gentle mother-in-law suffered a horrible death from liver cancer; my father at age 62, without any warning, died of a heart attack; our infant son, Gavin Ward Glanz, died after a completely normal pregnancy and birth; our St. Bernard puppy, "Nanna," had a heart attack during a simple surgery and died; and I found a lump in my breast. With each consecutive tragedy, I realized more and more my complete helplessness to save those I loved.

During that devastating time, I came to two decisions that have impacted my life to the very depths of my being:

1. I was hurting so much that I knew no one could ever hurt me so deeply again in my life. As a result, *I decided that I would never again try to be something or someone I was not, just to please others.* I vowed I would be completely authentic for the rest of my life, even if what I believed and felt was different from what others wanted to hear. To this very day I am the same person on the platform as I am off the platform, and I have begged my friends and family to challenge me immediately if they ever see this changing. Consequently, what I share with my audiences is not just a job or simply a presentation. It is authentically how I live my life, and I believe the truth of the message I share with my whole heart and soul. (Can you tell that, even as you read this book?)

2. In my grief, I powerfully experienced the belief that *"Every day is a gift."* Up to that point, I had been able to plan my life, and because I worked hard, I was able to achieve all the lofty goals I had set for myself. However, I quickly learned that I am *not* in control and that I must be grateful for each day of life and live it to the fullest. During my darkest time, a friend gave me a book by Jess Lair titled *I Ain't Much, Baby, But I'm All I've Got!* In the book he talks about living five minutes at a time. There were many days when the depression was so great that I couldn't even face surviving until noon; however, with prayer, I could always get through five minutes. This experience taught me the gift of living fully in the present. When I am with you, I am completely and totally with you, and although I do some planning, I know deep in my heart that the only surety I have is this immediate moment.

The quote from Elisabeth Kübler-Ross's at the beginning of this idea has deeply touched my heart, not only because of my life, but also as a reminder of the lives of others. *Everyone* has experienced pain and suffering in ways we cannot even imagine, and as we interact with other human beings, we must always keep that thought in mind. Sometimes we are blessed to be able to hear their stories; however, other times we can only acknowledge how little we really know of the experiences of their lives and treat them with kindness and respect even if they don't "deserve" it. I recently left this thought on my voice mail, *"Be kind. Everyone you meet is carrying something."*

► TIPS FOR IMPLEMENTATION

If you are going through a difficult time in your life, or if you have a loved one who is suffering, hold onto the thought that no matter how awful the situation may be now, good can eventually come from it if we can open ourselves to God's love and the love of those around us. We must be gentle with ourselves—it took me almost five years to be nearly "whole" again—yet I could never be the person I am today nor do the work I am doing that I know is changing lives if it had not been for that pain and suffering. In the midst of your pain or the pain of others, always remember, **BEAUTIFUL PEOPLE DO NOT JUST HAPPEN!** And when you are blessed to meet one of those "beautiful people," never feel envious or inadequate. Remember they, too, have suffered, so ask to hear their story. You will be more beautiful as a result.

(As a postscript, my dear husband of 33 years died of cancer five years ago; I recently made a move from Illinois to Florida, leaving everything familiar behind; and all of my children have since moved to the states of Washington and Oregon, about as far away as they could possibly be! However, I continue, even in my loneliness, to be thankful for each day and for my precious work of bringing new hope to organizations all over the world. I treasure all the beautiful people I have met along the way.)

Think about all the beautiful people you have met in your work. They did not become beautiful without times of pain, so be gentle to yourself and others as you face struggles in your life

You, too, can be beautiful!

27

Work on a Community Project

▶ THE IDEA

Whenever you can work together as a team on a project bigger than your organization, you are creating a special spirit of sharing and caring. This spirit will positively impact not only the way your team works together on the project but also how you work together to serve your customers. A side benefit is that your customers will appreciate what your team is doing to help your community, and the good PR will bring new customers to your door, so everybody wins.

▶ THE IDEA IN ACTION

The city of Harlan, Iowa, my hometown, completed a marvelous community project that involved local organizations and businesses, citizens, and even children. They built a "Dream Playground." This project was spearheaded by a single person, Mike Kolbe, the advertising manager for the *Harlan Tribune*, who made the dream playground come true. Everyone, regardless of age, was encouraged to work on it, and in the five days of building, over 600 people of all ages worked.

The playground was funded by donations from businesses and individuals as well as fund-raisers, including several run by the children of the community. In the "Coins for Kids" drive, they decorated collection cans and grocery sacks with pictures and "advertisements" for their new playground. These were used by the local stores to encourage people to make donations.

During the building process, everyone who volunteered got jobs. When the project was completed, the whole community held a celebration. That project created more community spirit than anything they have ever done—and they have a wonderful playground to show for it!

What police officers are actually doing for all
that time when they've got you pulled over.

When organizations meet their customers' quality demands
and also are seen as unique in their customers' eyes,
they have better customer-retention rates,
deeper customer relationships, better gross revenues
and margins, and are more profitable. In short,
organizations gain strategic advantage
by focusing on customer retention and creating value.

RON ZEMKE, AUTHOR,
THE SERVICE EDGE

► TIPS FOR IMPLEMENTATION

Some organizations participate in holiday projects to help others less fortunate in the community; others take on a project for Habitat for Humanity, where they build houses for the homeless in their communities. Another idea is to put together teams to volunteer at a humane society, to read to children in inner-city schools, or to visit nursing homes.

What I particularly loved about the Iowa project was that they planned jobs for all ages—people with carpentry or building skills built platforms, set poles, and put towers together; those with artistic talent created a replica of the Shelby County Courthouse; the children under age 10 were assigned jobs such as sanding boards, soaping screws, picking up scraps and trash, and carrying gravel for the playground; those from 10 to 18 got to hammer, carry lumber, and work with the adults. Stores in the area sent in food and drinks for the workers, and older residents baked cookies and bars for snacks.

Mike said, "The community spirit was a joy to see! We got to work with people we've never known before. Lawyers, farmers, and young children worked right next to one another." In planning a project for your organization, consider one where every employee and perhaps even their families can be involved. And remember, this project only took one person with enthusiasm to get it started. Never give up your dream!

28

"Every Customer Is a Gift"

▶ THE IDEA

As you interact with customers today, remember that each one of them is a gift to you and your organization. If it weren't for them, your organization would not exist and you would not have a job!

▶ THE IDEA IN ACTION

Earlier I shared this poem with you:

> YESTERDAY IS HISTORY.
>
> TOMORROW IS A MYSTERY.
>
> TODAY IS A GIFT.
>
> THAT'S WHY WE CALL IT "THE PRESENT."

Every day *is* a gift, and, likewise, every customer with whom we interact is a gift. Sometimes it seems that the customers are a bother because they keep us from getting our paperwork done, or they are constantly complaining about something. However, when

"Before you go, Mr. Gertman, we'd like you to fill out this customer satisfaction card to let us know how we can better serve you."

we remember to be grateful for each and every customer, we can begin to create a relationship that will lead to customer loyalty. When your customers know that you *really* appreciate them and their business, they will want to do more business with your organization, and that means job security for you!

List some of your favorite customers, both internal and external:

_____

_____

_____

_____

_____

_____

_____

_____

_____

Have you ever considered them as "gifts"? How might you demonstrate to them this week that you do?

► TIPS FOR IMPLEMENTATION

As a reminder that each customer is a gift, you may want to keep a small wrapped present in your work area. All gifts are special, just as each customer is special. Another client of mine has printed on each person's paycheck "This paycheck brought to you by our customers" as a reminder of how precious their customers are. As you create relationships on the human level with your customers, both internal and external, you are "opening" the gift of their uniqueness, getting to know and serve them.

29

Always Anticipate the Customers' Needs

▶ **THE IDEA**

Everyone in our world today seems pressed for time, so one of the ways you can most delight your customers is to anticipate what some of their future needs may be, give them suggestions of ways to meet those needs, and help save them valuable time.

▶ **THE IDEA IN ACTION**

Always put yourself in your customers' shoes. Think about their lives and how they may use the product or service you are offering them. Then think about what else they may need to get the full value or benefit from the product or service. For example, I have been really grateful when I have purchased items that require batteries (especially children's toys for a special occasion), and the salesperson has reminded me that I need them and has even gone to another department to get them for me. Can you imagine how it feels when your child opens a birthday gift she has been wanting for months and it won't work because it doesn't have batteries?

YOU HAVE REACHED OUR 800 NUMBER. IF YOU ARE A PREFERRED ACCOUNT, DIAL " W-E- L-O-V-E- Y-O-U" NOW. IF YOU ARE A REGULAR ACCOUNT, DIAL "S-O- W-H-A-T" NOW. IF YOU HAVE A COMPLAINT, DIAL "D-O-R-K" NOW.

Reprinted with permission from *The Creative Commumicator*.

Likewise, when I order something from a catalog, often accessories pictured are not included with the item or sometimes the item needs a special accessory that I don't know about, and I am always grateful when the customer service representative suggests that I may want to order them now. Recently I ordered a lovely voile dress from a catalog. The rep said, "Oh, you're going to love that dress. However, even though it's lined, I have seen it on, and it really needs a long slip underneath. They are very hard to find, I know, so I am wondering if you'd like to order the one we have in our lingerie catalog." That person not only anticipated my needs and saved me a great deal of time searching for an item, but she also knew her merchandise so well that she could offer a solution!

▶ TIPS FOR IMPLEMENTATION

The key to anticipation is to always see the situation from the customer's perspective. What else may he or she need to make this product or service useful? What other product or service would enhance or complement the product or service the customer has asked for? Or what might be even a better product or service for that particular customer than what he or she requested? Remember that they don't know your business like you do. Never view anticipation of the customer's needs as "cross selling," which, to many of us, has a negative, pushy connotation. Rather view it as helping the customer save time and get the best value from his or her purchase.

30

Whenever You Can, Offer the Customers Options

► **THE IDEA**

Whenever we offer others options, we are respecting them as individuals and allowing them to make their own choices.

► **THE IDEA IN ACTION**

My children are all very independent persons and have wanted to make their own choices since they were very young. One of the ways I solved the battle of getting dressed in the morning was to put out three different outfits, always making a big deal out of letting them choose which one they wanted to wear. They may not have been thrilled with any of the three, but at least they had a choice. (This way I also avoided the humiliation Moms can experience when their precious little ones go to school in completely unmatched outfits!)

"Unfortunately, ma'am, the fire department can't get here for another two hours. However, a gentleman at the top has volunteered to slide down and try to knock you free."

Customers, too, are independent and want to have things their own way. Often our policies and procedures make the customer feel powerless. Think about how you feel when you feel powerless. For most of us, it brings about feelings of anger, resentment, revenge, and helplessness. These feelings, unfortunately, often get expressed to the customer service rep. One of the ways we can show respect to our customers and give them feelings of being in control is to offer them options or alternatives. Then whatever action is taken becomes their choice. Just like my children, they may not be thrilled with any of the choices, but at least they do not feel completely helpless, and they have some say in the outcome. Think about situations that come up over and over with customers and list several options you might offer for each. The option may be as simple as how they would like an item shipped or as complicated as several different choices to resolve a difficulty.

For example, when a vendor in another city lost the master of one of my audio compact discs and could not make the copies I needed on time for a very important client, instead of just saying he could not do what I needed, he gave me several options:

1. He would contact the company that taped the session and pay for a new master and then ship the copies overnight to the client at his expense.
2. I could take a copy I had to a local vendor to have it copied, and he would pay the cost.
3. He would copy another CD master of mine at his expense and send it to the customer with an apology and an assurance that they would receive the original order in two weeks.

Needless to say, even though he had caused me a huge problem, he offered me options that more than satisfied me and ensured that I would be an ongoing loyal customer!

SITUATION:

OPTIONS:

SITUATION:

OPTIONS:

SITUATION:

OPTIONS:

▶ TIPS FOR IMPLEMENTATION

The key to offering options is to think "out of the box." Get your creative juices going and find new, creative ways to solve customers' problems. Often an unusual, creative solution will surprise and delight your customers and will also diffuse their anger and feelings of helplessness. Always focus on what you *can* do, not on what you can't do!

31

Inform the Customers When You Have Gone Out of Your Way for Them

▶ THE IDEA

Often customer service professionals do extra things for customers or go out of their way to help them behind the scenes, and the customers never know of the professionals' actions. Even though we are often told to do good things in secret, in the business world it is important to let the customers know how hard we have tried to help them. Otherwise, they may think that we just did enough to get by.

▶ THE IDEA IN ACTION

I mentioned earlier a dress that I wanted and a salesperson who offered me options. That was the end of the story! The beginning of the story was that I saw a particular dress in a store catalog, and

"Unfortunately, ma'am, our fitting rooms are being renovated. But if you'll just step behind this clothing rack, Betty and Rowena will be happy to stand guard for you while you change."

I knew it was simply made for me! (I know my women readers will understand what I mean.) It was my favorite color, red, and it was a rather unusual style, something that I search for since I am a professional speaker and want to provide visual interest for my clients. When I called the store, I explained all this with enthusiasm, and the salesperson realized just how much I wanted that dress. She got excited, too, sharing in my delight at finding just the perfect thing and said she would try to find it for me. She said she was really busy right then and would call back at 10:00 a.m. the next day.

Precisely at 10:00 a.m. the phone rang, and from the moment I answered, I knew she did not have good news. Her voice was filled with sadness, and she said, "Barbara, I know how very much you wanted that red dress. I spent all yesterday afternoon on the telephone calling. I called 18 different stores, and nine of them were in other states. No one in the country has the dress in your size. I am so sorry to have to disappoint you, but I really tried my hardest to find it for you, and I just had no luck." Then she offered me the options I told you about earlier.

The important thing here is that she *told* me how hard she had tried in very specific detail, and I also knew that she really cared about me and finding that dress. If she had simply said, "I tried to find the dress for you, but no one has it in your size," I would never have known how much she had done for me, and I probably would have been upset with both her and the store for advertising a dress that they didn't have. However, in this case, I wasn't thrilled because I still did not get my dress, but I also wasn't angry and I remained a loyal customer because I knew how hard she had tried to please me.

Nothing liberates our greatness like the desire to help,
the desire to serve.

MARIANNE WILLIAMSON

▶ TIPS FOR IMPLEMENTATION

Always explain in *specific detail* the steps you have taken to help the customers. Don't ever assume they know what you did for them; always *tell* them, because what you are telling them is that you cared enough to go out of your way to try to help them. They will appreciate that effort on a human level even if you are not able to meet their business need.

32

Manage by Wandering Around

▶ **THE IDEA**

For many years we have heard about MBWA (also known as "Manage by Wandering Around") as a management tool. Today, because of low morale, fear, and a loss of trust in most organizations, it is even more important for the manager to be out with her or his employees for part of the day and not simply sitting in an office. Only by rebuilding trust and teamwork will most organizations survive. The employees need to feel that their manager is on their side and supporting them, not waiting for them to do something wrong. And, if you are an employee, encourage your manager to spend time with you and better understand your work by asking him or her to help you with something or ask his or her opinion about a change or a new process. Team members can reach out to one another and learn about each other's jobs to create an atmosphere of sharing and cooperation.

▶ THE IDEA IN ACTION

Spend time out in the field with employees. Ask them how you can help make their jobs easier. Work alongside them. Even let them teach you what they do. For example, Southwest Airlines has a mandate that every manager must spend one-third of his or her time in direct touch with employees and customers—for example, throwing bags, taking reservations, or acting as a flight attendant—to create a stronger feeling of teamwork.

The chairperson of financial operations of a local company makes it a point at some time before the end of the day to walk through all the suites the company occupies. He talks with employees, jokes with them, and asks how he can help. His simple action helps to create an atmosphere of informality and trust in that organization.

"If you don't mind, Mr. Morris, I'd like to get one more photo with you, me, and some of the ambulance attendants, and then we'll get you right over to X-ray."

A senior manager of a large bank spends one day a month as a teller. He at random chooses a branch, surprises the employees that morning, and buys them all pizza for lunch. They have to teach him how to do their job, and he says it's the hardest work he does all month!

Another excellent idea is to pass out employees' paychecks personally so you can thank them and even learn all their names if it is a large organization.

Here are some guidelines to use as you walk around. These ideas apply to *any* employee who wants to learn more and participate more fully in the work of the whole team:

- Don't take your cell phone or your PDA.
- Do more listening than talking.
- Make eye contact.
- Ask questions.
- Be honest.
- Show appreciation.
- Do it regularly.

Questions you might ask them are: "What can I start doing to make your job easier?" and "What can I quit doing to make your job easier?" Or, "What is a concern you have about your job?" Employees can ask the very same questions of their coworkers or even their boss!

► **TIPS FOR IMPLEMENTATION**

How often are you out on the frontlines if you're a manager? Plan a strategy so that you make it a part of your goal to spend a certain portion of your time with employees and customers. For example, if you manage a call center, how long has it been since *you* spent an hour on the phones with customers? For those of you who hope to be managers some day, remember not to ever lose understanding and empathy for the job from which you came.

Former Secretary of Labor Robert B. Reich said recently, "For six months now, I've been visiting the workplaces of America, administering a simple test. I call it the 'pronoun test.' I ask front-line workers a few general questions about the company. If the answers I get back describe the company in terms like 'they' and 'them,' then I know it's one kind of company. If the answers are put in terms like 'we' or 'us,' then I know it's a different kind of company."

33

Know Why Customers Are Unhappy with Your Organization

▶ **THE IDEA**

In any organization it is important to study the reasons why customers are unhappy. In the private sector, unhappy customers can simply leave and go to the competition. In the public sector, even if they can't leave, they can do many things such as bad-mouthing the agency, withholding their votes, going to the press, making it extremely difficult for the government employee to serve them, and/or pressuring legislators when they are disgruntled. All of these actions hurt the organization.

▶ **THE IDEA IN ACTION**

My friend Michael LeBoeuf, the author of many best-selling business books, performed a study on why customers stop doing business with an organization in the private sector or sabotage the organization in the public sector. Here are the results:

- 3 percent move away.
- 5 percent develop other friendships.
- 9 percent leave for competitive reasons.
- 14 percent are dissatisfied with the product or service.
- 68 percent leave (sabotage in the public sector) because of an attitude of *indifference* toward the customer by the owner, manager, or an employee.

As you can see, your organization actually has some control over *92 percent* of the reasons customers stop doing business with you or bad-mouth your organization. More importantly, you have *direct* control over how you treat each customer, accounting for 68 percent of those who leave or sabotage your organization. This study highlights in a powerful way the importance of each and every one of your employees in their interactions with customers. "Indifferent" treatment isn't even being rude; it is simply not caring. So, showing the customer how much you care about them and their needs at every level in the organization will make the greatest difference in building customer loyalty and impacting your bottom line!

► TIPS FOR IMPLEMENTATION

Share these statistics with every employee in your organization so they will know the impact their individual behavior has on the entire company. Also interview unhappy customers to find out what upset them and try to fix those things, especially if you see patterns or groupings of complaints. You already learned some sam-

**After trying for 25 minutes to get their check,
Ed was finally able to get their waiter's attention.**

ple interview questions to ask them in idea 15 "Hold Focus Groups, Part One." Often an unhappy customer who is shown that someone does, indeed, care can be a more loyal customer as a result. Above all, remember that it costs five times as much to get a new customer as to keep an old one. Do everything in your power to keep and value those old customers!

34

Honor Customer Complaints

► **THE IDEA**

> *It's critical to keep the company's*
> *"ear to the ground."*
> *I know something is wrong*
> *if I hear no complaints.*
> *Complaints are my assurance that customers*
> *want to make an imperfect situation better.*

ANONYMOUS GENERAL MANAGER

In my classes on "Building a Customer-Focused Organization," I often ask participants how many of them like a customer complaint. When few, if any, hands go up, I tell them I am going to "whack" their thinking—I want them to *honor* and *value* customer complaints.

"The plumber said he ran into some unexpected problems and will be back sometime next week."

▶ THE IDEA IN ACTION

Research has shown that only 4 to 6 percent of our unhappy customers bother to complain. The other 92 to 96 percent simply take their business elsewhere in the private sector or bad-mouth and sabotage the organization in the public sector. We also know that an unhappy customer today tells 15 to 20 other people even when they don't tell us!

Therefore, it is important to reframe your thinking about complaints. First of all, if only 4 to 6 percent of your customers take time to complain, they really are your *partners* because they are helping you learn what is breaking down in your organization. Also, by letting you know their concern, they are giving you an opportunity to fix it and ultimately create a loyal customer.

Another reason to value complaints is that if one customer is complaining and you know that 92 percent of your customers never even bother, you can be pretty sure that more than just this one customer is upset by whatever problem they are bringing to your attention.

Honor customer complaints as *opportunities*—opportunities to learn what is impacting the customers in a negative way and opportunities to create loyal customers by fixing the problem quickly and creatively.

▶ TIPS FOR IMPLEMENTATION

Instead of griping about customers who complain, honor them. You might even create "Complaint of the Month or Week" and then showcase the ways you resolved the complaint to highlight the importance of listening with compassion and concern and finding creative solutions. Remember, if unhappy customers are not complaining to you, they *are* telling everyone else about their complaints!

35

Do Just a Little Bit Extra for Each Customer

▶ **THE IDEA**

Whenever you do something extra for a customer, you make him or her feel special and cared for. You have gone out of your way just for that person, and doing so is what creates loyal customers. There is a saying that there is a lot less traffic on the extra mile! When you get your creative juices going and truly focus on each individual customer as a human being, not only will you build a long-term relationship, but that customer will also tell the story over and over to others.

▶ **THE IDEA IN ACTION**

If you are always thinking about what is best for the customer and what special little thing you can do to help him or her, you will never be perceived as selling. You will be serving the customer. When a telemarketer for a long-distance service called a colleague recently, she said she was taken aback because he didn't seem to be reading a script. He asked her several very sincere questions about

"Your fettuccine calamari is going to be another 10 or 15 minutes."

her business, and when he found out that she owned a communications company, he asked her if she had read an article that had appeared that week in one of the business magazines on communications. When she replied that she hadn't, he offered to fax it to her. She said she was blown away that he would offer to do that.

She ended up switching her service because he went out of his way to help her in her business.

Several years ago, I was meeting a client at a downtown hotel for a dinner meeting. I do not often drive in downtown Chicago; however, I was coming from a previous appointment, so I had no choice. The doorman was very gracious in helping us choose a place to eat and in giving us directions. After dinner when I returned my client to the hotel, I needed directions back to the expressway. The doorman gave me verbal directions and then said, "I will feel more comfortable if I give you a map just in case you get lost." He then went back into the hotel and brought out a map which he highlighted for me. He even offered to call my husband to tell him that I was on my way home. As I left, he reminded me, "Don't forget to lock your doors!" That gentleman went far out of his way to make me feel safe and cared for—and I wasn't even a guest in the hotel!

► TIPS FOR IMPLEMENTATION

It is fun to always be thinking of extra little things you can do for the customer. If you truly focus on customers and not what's in it for you and listen with an open mind and a big heart, you will always find ways to delight them. Give just a little bit more than is expected, and you will create loyal customers!

36

Take an Internal Customer to Lunch

▶ THE IDEA

Remember that customers, whether internal or external, want to be "in on things," and part of what makes someone feel special is attention. One of the best ways to create an atmosphere of loyalty, trust and sharing is to take an internal customer to lunch.

▶ THE IDEA IN ACTION

Invite at least one person who supports your department or group to breakfast and another to lunch each week. Since sharing a meal is something we all do with friends, it is a perfect time to create rapport and build a relationship apart from your usual interactions.

On the human level you can learn more about one another's families, hobbies, and interests. (Don't forget to ask to see children's pictures!) On the business level, ask them for their ideas to improve the organization, where they see barriers occurring, and

"You want your coffee warmed up a bit?"

thank them for being on your team. You will be amazed at the loyalty and team feeling you will create by building these relationships outside of the office.

Both employees and managers can put this idea into action. One company randomly selects 10 employees a week to have lunch with each senior manager on Friday of that week until they have worked through the entire company. Other companies ask employees to request the manager with whom they would most like to share a meal. Whether you are a manager or not, you can call one or two people with whom you work each week and invite them to a "sharing" lunch.

▶ TIPS FOR IMPLEMENTATION

If you are a manager, you might give employees a choice if they would like to have lunch alone with you or if they would be more comfortable in a small group. It is important, however, that everyone has a chance to have this experience with their manager and not just a "chosen" few. Otherwise it will be a demotivator in the organization. If you are an employee, ask those internal customers whom you do not know well to share coffee or a meal, and that will help create more understanding and teamwork across the company.

37

Are You Friendly?

▶ **THE IDEA**

You can research what your customers think is friendly treatment. Focus on behaviors that are measurable, observable, and capable of being replicated. Begin by writing down several behaviors that *you* like when you are the customer. Then ask your customers for their input: What do you expect a "friendly" employee to do?

▶ **THE IDEA IN ACTION**

When a large bank in North America asked its customers that question, they found there were four behaviors that customers felt represented "friendly" behavior:

1. Greeting the customer with a smile.
2. Using the customer's name.
3. Saying one thing other than the business at hand (such things as comments about the weather, a compliment, a human-level question, a comment about a current event).
4. Thanking the customer.

Reprinted with permission from *The Creative Commumicator*.

Are these things that you do with your customers? Keep a list of them near your workstation or desk, and each time you interact with a customer mentally check them off. These behaviors are observable (someone else can watch you and check which ones you did); they are measurable (you can keep track of how many times you did one, two, three, or four of these things with customers), and they can be repeated (the meaning of each behavior is clear, and each person can exhibit these behaviors over and over).

▶ TIPS FOR IMPLEMENTATION

One way to have fun with these behaviors as well as keeping an awareness of them is to have a contest of who can use them with customers the most. The bank I mentioned above, at the beginning of each month, gave each teller and personal banker a basket of 25 silver dollars to put at his or her station. Each basket had a little card that read: "We want to be a friendly bank. Our customers have told us that these are the four things that represent 'friendliness' to them [the list was included]. We are trying hard to be friendly in every interaction; however, we need your help. If one of our employees does not do each of the four things on this list, please take a silver dollar from the basket as a reminder to all of us."

At the end of the month, each teller got to keep all the money left in his or her basket. Not only was this fun for the customers, but it also was a special bonus for friendly employees!

38

Think Like a Customer

▶ THE IDEA

When you put yourself in your customer's place, you can better understand what your customer wants and what will delight him or her.

▶ THE IDEA IN ACTION

Think of a time when you were treated really well as the customer of some organization—for example, a restaurant, gas station, telephone company, bank, or grocery store. What did that employee or employees *do* to create a positive experience for you? Write down on paper the *actual behaviors* of the employee that made you feel special:

- _____
  _____
- _____
  _____
- _____
  _____
- _____
  _____

Ask several of your coworkers to do the same exercise. Then compare your lists. Do you see some of the same behaviors repeated?

Ask yourself, "Can I do these things with my customers?" If those behaviors created positive experiences for you and your friends, they will also most likely create positive experiences for your customers, too.

▶ TIPS FOR IMPLEMENTATION

Be much more aware of the service you receive as a customer, and when you are dazzled by an employee, not only tell him or her (or their boss) but also remember what they did and try to repeat those behaviors with your own customers.

> *A sale is not something you pursue;*
> *it is something that happens to you*
> *while you are immersed in serving your customer.*
>
> UNKNOWN

39

Four Things Customers Want

▶ **THE IDEA**

British Airways did a study in 1973 that has been repeated hundreds and hundreds of times, and the results have been the same every time. They found that there were four things all their customers wanted:

1. *Friendly, caring service*—a focus on the person as a human being.
2. *Flexibility*—they want you to jiggle the system for them.
3. *Problem solving*, and they want it by the first person they speak to.
4. *Recovery* when the organization makes a mistake. There are three parts to recovery—*apologize* sincerely, *fix* the "Mis-Take," *do something extra*, and then follow up to make sure the customer is happy.

Despite their popularity, many of the fancy new mall hair salons just don't have the personal touch of the old neighborhood barber shops.

► THE IDEA IN ACTION

If these are the four things our customers want, let's look at ways we can achieve these behaviors in our jobs each day. Take a few moments to get your creative juices going, consider each of these four questions individually, and write down some things you can do in each area to please your customers:

1. How can you show friendly, caring service?

   _____

   _____

2. How can you demonstrate flexibility?

   _____

   _____

3. How can you problem solve for the customer even if it isn't your job?

_____

_____

4. How can you recover when you have made a "Mis-Take"?

_____

_____

Share the ideas you have written down with several coworkers.

► **TIPS FOR IMPLEMENTATION**

Keep these four things posted in your workspace and look at them every day. Once a week at a staff meeting, share ideas of how you have met these customer needs in creative ways. These behaviors will lead to loyal customers *and* job assurance for you!

40

Manage from the Heart

▶ **THE IDEA**

Ask yourself the question, "Am I managing my people on both the human and the Business levels?" Unless you are truly taking both levels into account in your management style, my guess is that your employees are not living up to their full potential and productivity. This same principle is also true in working with customers. Their interactions need to be managed on both the business and the human levels.

▶ **THE IDEA IN ACTION**

Hyler Bracy in his book *Managing from the Heart* says that all employees (and, I believe, all customers) are crying out for the behaviors that make up the acronym "HEART":

- *Hear and understand me.* It is critically important to listen to both spoken and unspoken needs of both employees and customers. Use empathy to "walk in their shoes" and to try to understand how they feel. Doing this will make the difference between having a happy employee or customer and having one who feels betrayed, angry, misunderstood, and uncared for.

- *Even if you disagree with me, please don't make me wrong.* Think about the "Way It Is" model. It says that with anything there is:
  - The way *you* see it.
  - The way *I* see it.
  - The way it *really* is.

  Just because two people see things differently does not mean that one of them is right and the other is wrong; it simply means they have a different view. Communicating with each other and allowing each person to fully explain the way he or she sees it will help keep a feeling of respect in the interaction. And, even if you decide to do it *your* way because you are the boss or the person in charge, that still does not mean that the other person is wrong. You have simply decided to do it your way.

- *Acknowledge the greatness within me.* There is a seed of greatness in every person, and we must keep looking until we find it. Everyone needs appreciation and encouragement, and finding and acknowledging other people's strength and searching for the uniqueness of their characters indicates a deep respect for them as human beings.

- *Remember to look for my loving intentions.* We have a choice every day of our lives—to live in faith or to live in fear.

I choose to live in faith and to believe the best of people, at least until they prove me wrong. Remember the self-fulfilling prophecy, you get what you look for? If you truly look for loving intentions, I sincerely believe you will find them!

"For her twelve years of service as a data processor and for keypunching in 3,789 records in one eight-hour shift, please welcome our employee of the year, Peggy Neal!"

- *Tell me the truth with compassion.* This is yet another application of the Human Business Model as it relates to coaching or giving customers information. You can share difficult or unwanted information on the *Business* level; however, *you can do it in a kind and caring way* on the Human level. I often ask my audiences, "Have you ever been told 'No' in a kind and caring way?" (Isn't that what we do almost every day as parents?)

All of these behaviors fall on the human level and lead to caring, sharing relationships and the rebuilding of trust, whether it is with an employee or a customer.

▶ TIPS FOR IMPLEMENTATION

Meet with a group of employees in your organization and discuss what each of these unconscious requests for HEART means

1. to employees
2. in terms of your actions as a manager
3. to customers

41

The Four Steps of Recovery

▶ **THE IDEA**

One of the four things our customers want is for us to recover when we have made a "Mis-Take." When we are ill, the word "recovery" means to get better or back to normal. Likewise, when we have disappointed a customer, we need to get back to normal with them.

▶ **THE IDEA IN ACTION**

There are four steps in the recovery process:

1. *Apologize sincerely.* Make sure that your apology is not flip or forced.
2. *Fix it.* Do whatever is necessary to fix the "Mis-Take." You may have to do some creative thinking to find what you *can* do or to offer options of alternatives. It is always good if you can give the customer a choice: "We can do this or this or this."
3. *Do something extra.* This is the step in the process that can

really delight your customer. If you are creative and do something that surprises them, they will not only tell many other people, but they will also be more loyal to your organization than if the "Mis-Take" never happened. Recently when I angrily complained about a voice mail service that had not been fixed after three calls and spending a great deal of time lost in "voice mail jail," the customer service rep, after he had fixed the problem, asked what he could do to make me feel better. I asked him what he thought, and he replied, "How about if I make this month's service free?" I was dazzled—I never would have thought of that. His action kept me from changing my service, and it impacted my bottom line since this was a business line. My frustration quickly changed to delight!

4. *Follow up.* The same rep wrote me a letter afterward apologizing for all the trouble I'd had, gave me his name and number so that I would have a contact in that huge, bureaucratic organization if I had a problem again, and said he hoped he had resolved my problem in a way that would keep me a customer of theirs for a long time. And you know what? He did, and I am! (I also wrote a letter complimenting him to his boss.)

▶ TIPS FOR IMPLEMENTATION

Remember that a "Mis-Take" can become an opportunity to create a loyal customer. You must, however, act quickly (usually within 72 hours) and creatively to dazzle a customer. Whenever you can give something extra to the customer, she or he feels atonement for the "Mis-Take," and it becomes a great story for that person to share with friends!

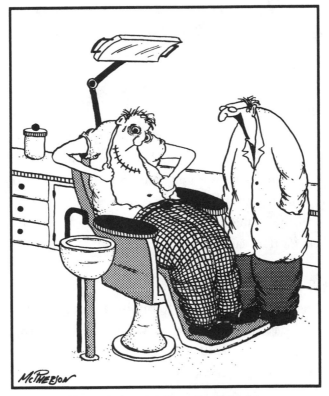

"That wisdom tooth on the right side was giving me a tough time. So I had to get at it from a different angle."

42

Happy Employees Create Happy Customers

▶ **THE IDEA**

Have you ever seen a company with *unhappy* employees who had *happy* customers? I haven't! Employees need managers who can empathize with their stress and pain and who honestly try to create an environment in which everyone feels valued and respected despite all the changes going on around them. Then they can be their best for their customers.

▶ **THE IDEA IN ACTION**

According to an article by Kenneth Kovach in *Employment Relations Today,* when employees were asked what they valued most about their jobs in 1946, 1981, and again in 1995, these were the top three things employees reported:

1. Interesting work
2. Full appreciation for the work they'd done
3. A feeling of being "in" on things

At The National Academy of Mall Security Guards

Each of these motivators relates to an element of the type of caring, spirited workplace managers can create for their employees. The best news is that these things do not cost any money, and you have lots of control over them as a manager. Take a few moments and list some ways you can implement each of these three things with your employees:

INTERESTING WORK:

_____

_____

_____

FULL APPRECIATION:

_____

_____

_____

FEELING OF BEING IN ON THINGS:

_____

_____

_____

▶ **TIPS FOR IMPLEMENTATION**

Post this list where you can see it in your office every day. Get together with several other managers and brainstorm even more ways you can creatively help meet employees' needs in each of these areas.

43

Hold Grapevine Sessions

► **THE IDEA**

Because one of the things all employees want from their jobs is a "feeling of being in on things," it is important to communicate honestly, openly, regularly, and in ways that surprise and delight your employees. One way to offset gossip and rumors is to hold informal, spontaneous information-sharing meetings.

► **THE IDEA IN ACTION**

Hold informal "grapevine sessions" to control the flow of the rumor mill. These open discussions can be held either on a regular basis or can be called by any employee. Give employees permission to come to a senior manager whenever the rumor mill is overflowing and ask the manager to call a grapevine meeting. The meeting must be immediate (sometime that day) and open to all. Hold it in a place like the cafeteria where employees feel comfortable.

Managers must be prepared to listen and to be completely truthful and open. Even when they can't share specific informa-

**Most employees found that playing the new game in
the cafeteria was a great way to relieve stress.**

tion, they can honestly explain why and when it will be available.
For example, tell employees everything you possibly can, including
even bad news. Over and over again, employees are saying, "Tell us
the truth, even the bad news. We can handle it. What we can't
handle is the fear and uncertainty of not knowing." Above all,
never lie to employees.

When a local company went public recently, the CEO made sure they communicated even when they *couldn't* communicate. When things had to be kept secret by law, he called meetings to explain the reasons why they couldn't tell employees more, and he prepared them for what they would see so that when private meetings were held, they weren't afraid. He anticipated their concerns and responded to events like stock fluctuations immediately with either a corporate wide e-mail message or a voice mail message that explained what was happening. This CEO built trust during a time when trust could easily have been lost.

▶ **TIPS FOR IMPLEMENTATION**

Establish some ground rules for your grapevine sessions, such as

- Only one person can talk at a time.
- No one is allowed to blame or threaten.
- Every question is legitimate.

This is a forum to get issues out on the table and to share information. In order to rebuild trust, employees must be free to ask questions and to contribute their opinions and feelings. Set a time limit of no more than 30 to 45 minutes, and allow free-flowing questions and answers. Doing so will do more to clear the air and rid the company of unproductive gossip than any other intervention.

44

Stay Calm with a Difficult Customer

► **THE IDEA**

No matter how upset a customer is, always stay calm and focus on that customer and not on yourself.

► **THE IDEA IN ACTION**

1. *Breathe deeply.* Doing so will relax you and help you to gain control of your feelings.

2. *Listen and empathize.* Put yourself in the customer's shoes.

3. *Remember the customer's human need.* Even if you can't, with creative thinking, meet the business need of the customer, you can *always* meet her or his human need for dignity and understanding.

4. *Let the person vent.* Sometimes the customer simply needs to let off steam to someone. Agree with him or her every chance you get, even if it is only a "yes," or "uh-huh." If you listen long enough without arguing, often the customer will

**"Stick the other end of this in your mouth
and say 'Ahh.'"**

run out of steam and end up apologizing to you or explaining that he or she has had a bad day.

5. Ask questions! Doing so buys you time to keep calm and puts the ball in their court.

6. *Don't take things personally.* When a customer is upset, he or she is upset with the organization or the circumstances, not

with you as an individual. Remember, *you are the organization* to that customer; he or she sees you as representing the whole rather than as an individual person. Keeping this in mind can help you stay unhooked in a negative interaction, because it is not about you, the human being, but rather about what has happened with the organization.

► TIPS FOR IMPLEMENTATION

Share these tips with everyone on your team, and then practice them. The best way is to practice at home first. If these techniques work there, when a family member is upset (and they will get upset from time to time), they are guaranteed to work with an angry customer!

45

A Dilemma to Discuss

▶ **THE IDEA**

Think about the situation described in this idea. It is a good one to discuss with your work team.

▶ **THE IDEA IN ACTION**

A receptionist in the Radiation Department of a large hospital recently told me about a situation that merits some discussion if you truly want to be a customer-focused organization. It was a quiet day, and an outpatient in a wheelchair had been waiting a long time for someone to take her down to the emergency room exit to have her family pick her up. No one was available to wheel her about 300 yards to the elevator and another 500 yards to the emergency room waiting area. Finally, the receptionist decided that he would take her down himself, and he left his station for a total of about three minutes.

Later his supervisor, who was very upset about the incident, told him, "You have no respect for authority." The employee answered, "I'm not here for you. I'm here to serve the patients."

From a service perspective, who was right in this situation?

**"This is what I get for requesting an
office with a window."**

▶ TIPS FOR IMPLEMENTATION

Who do you think was right? Were there any possible compromises
that might have made the situation more positive for all three
participants?

46

Create a Human-Level Database

▶ THE IDEA

When Baxter Labs conducted a worldwide survey to find out what they could do to make the workplace environment better for their employees, the top answer they got back worldwide was:

> To be respected as whole human beings with a life outside of work.

▶ THE IDEA IN ACTION

Start a "human-level" database in your organization. Collect information about the employees such as the following:

- Hobbies
- Whether the employees play an instrument, sing, draw, or speak a foreign language

- Special interests such as golf, bridge, and tennis
- Favorite sports and sports teams
- Books and movies they like
- Places they have traveled
- Where they grew up and where they went to school
- Organizations and support groups to which they belong

All of this information relates to what employees do in their free time, in their lives outside of work.

► TIPS FOR IMPLEMENTATION

Knowing personal information about your coworkers and staff becomes a terrific way to network internally, and research has shown that one of the greatest determinants for employee loyalty is having a good friend at work. Informal classes, support groups, travel groups, and perhaps even a company choir or band will spring up. People can find others to help them with problems both at work and at home, and the company will discover resources it never knew it had. Best of all, employees are seen as whole persons, not just workers!

> *Oh,*
> *if only we could see ourselves as our customers see us,*
> *comprehend the ways we dehumanize,*
> *demean, and demoralize them.*
> *The great news is that such insane stuff*
> *makes the teeniest good deed stand out.*
>
> TOM PETERS

47

Use Selective Agreement

▶ THE IDEA

When customers are really upset about something, they want a fight. They are so angry that they just want someone to argue with, so they may attack you personally as well as denigrating the organization. Your job is to remain calm, not take the insults personally, and to create empathy with the customer by finding things in what they say *that you can agree with*. This skill is called "selective agreement."

▶ THE IDEA IN ACTION

When you think about what is taught in tai chi or karate or even boxing, it is all about "rolling with the punches" and deflecting the attack. Students are taught never to stand firm but to move with the energy in a way that deflects it. Let's say that a very angry customer is attacking you and the organization through threats and verbal and sometimes even physical actions. Instead of becoming defensive and angry yourself, you can often defuse the customer's

"Unfortunately, Mrs. Dortford, our entire X-ray department is on strike. But if you'll just describe your pain in as much detail as possible, our staff sketch artist should be able to give us a fairly accurate drawing of the problem."

anger by finding some part of what he or she says that you can agree with. This throws the other person off balance because he or she is wanting and expecting you to fight back, which would escalate the customer's anger, and instead, you are agreeing with him or her.

Here are some things you can say in response to threats:

- "I agree that the situation was handled badly."
- "You are right—our lines are sometimes very long."
- "Yes, that person was not fully informed about our policies."
- "You are right. We did make a mistake."

▶ TIPS FOR IMPLEMENTATION

No matter how upset customers are, you can almost always find something in what they say that you can agree with. You may have to use this skill six or seven times, depending upon how upset the customer is, before he or she calms down enough for you to get to the business at hand. Using this strategy will keep you focused on responding positively and help you to stay more objective so you will not take the attack personally. If you can stay calm, sooner or later, the customer will run out of steam and often end up apologizing. Above all, when dealing with a difficult customer, *don't get hooked!*

My suggestion is to practice this skill at home first. I found it priceless in dealing with my teenagers when they thought I was the worst Mom in the whole world!

48

Use an Objective Measurement to Communicate the Seriousness of the Situation

▶ **THE IDEA**

Use a scale of 1 to 10. This tool can be used in giving feedback and coaching, in assessing the magnitude of the need when requesting work from an internal coworker, or in discussing the seriousness of an issue with a customer. It helps to objectively define how important the message or issue is and to keep things in perspective.

▶ **THE IDEA IN ACTION**

When you are discussing a problem with customers, ask them to rank how serious it really is on a scale of 1 to 10, with 1 being just

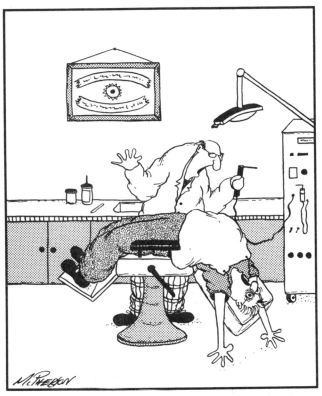

"Hey, look, I'm sorry that this gives you a migraine,
but it makes it a heck of a lot easier for me
to get to those upper molars."

a very small hitch in the works and 10 being a major complication in their lives. Often, when they are asked to do this, customers realize that their problem is really not all that great in the whole scheme of things. On the other hand, when it is of major concern to them, it will help you to react with the urgency they desire.

This skill is particularly valuable to use with internal customers when they need work completed by you and you are swamped with requests. Asking them on a scale of 1 to 10 how important it is to receive it within a certain time frame will help you to prioritize your work.

When coaching an employee, this process will allow them to understand how serious your feedback is. For example, you might say, "The feedback I am going to give you regarding your treatment of that last customer is only a 3 in terms of seriousness; however, because I want you to be the best you can be, it is important for you to see how you can improve your interaction with our customers." That numerical representation allows the employee to relax and know that he or she has not done anything seriously wrong. If, on the other hand, your manager tells you that the feedback she is going to give you is a 9 on the same scale, you had better listen carefully!

▶ TIPS FOR IMPLEMENTATION

Too often both internal and external customers as well as managers overreact to difficult or frustrating situations. Many times these occurrences are simply the "straw that broke the camel's back," to use a common expression, meaning that so many other things have gone wrong in their day or week that this is the final blow for them, and they simply explode. Asking them to rank the importance of the issue in their lives will help everyone to cope with more patience and understanding and to truly assess the seriousness of the problem.

49

Celebrate Any Good News You Can Find!

▶ THE IDEA

We need to focus more on *positives* in our organizations today. Use every opportunity you can to celebrate good news. Celebrate everything you can—meeting of short-term goals, the end of the budget process, winning grants or new customers, extraordinary work, safety successes, or even perfect attendance by your department for a month. We know that happy employees are more productive employees!

▶ THE IDEA IN ACTION

Hold a voluntary "Good News Hour" once a week for 30 minutes before the workday starts. Meet in the atrium, lobby, or the cafeteria of the building. Ask everyone to share good things that have happened in their lives, communities, and work during the last week. In organizations that have started this tradition, over 94 percent of the employees attend, and morale and productivity have been raised considerably. More laughter is being heard in the workplace, and people are feeling a deeper purpose in their work.

Another less time-consuming idea is to begin every meeting with three minutes of good news. By the way, this can occur in meetings in your schools, your communities, your churches, and service groups as well as in the workplace. Just ask anyone in the meeting to share any good thing that has happened in their homes, their community, their workplace, or the world.

When I ask clients about what most of their meetings are focused on, it is usually what is going wrong. We need to focus more on what is going *right*. Since I believe this so strongly, I have

"Congratulations, sir! You're the state's one-millionth speeder!"

clients all over the world begin every meeting with three minutes of good news to celebrate the positive things happening in their jobs and in their personal lives. They tell me that their meetings are shorter, more positive, and more productive and that people are coming *on time* because they don't want to miss the three minutes of good news! Best of all, people are sharing things that many times in their culture they were never able to share before. The only difficulty they find is *stopping* at just three minutes! When people have permission to share good news and begin to become aware of all the good things that are happening in their lives instead of focusing on the bad things, they get excited and want to share more and more.

▶ TIPS FOR IMPLEMENTATION

Pass the leadership of a Good News Hour session around. Don't make it a project of senior management but let it be a grassroots effort. Ask for a volunteer to facilitate each session or ask for a volunteer chairperson to coordinate the initial PR and location. After it gets started, it will take little or no maintenance. When you decide to begin all your meetings with three minutes of good news, you may need to model your good news first, but you will be amazed, once it gets started, what good things can happen in your meetings and then later on in your places of work as your employees begin to focus on what is going right.

50

Have a Thank Your Customers Day

► **THE IDEA**

One of the things we all crave is appreciation, so when you do something special to appreciate your customers, you are creating an even stronger relationship and building customer loyalty.

► **THE IDEA IN ACTION**

Here are several ways you can thank your customers that will surprise and delight them:

Celebrate All of Your Customers at One Time

Choose at least one day a year/month/week to have a customer appreciation day. Make it special and fun for the customer. Here are some ideas:

- *Decorate inside and out.* A driver's license facility in the state of Michigan decorates for every holiday to surprise and delight their customers. People drive out of their way to come to their office to enjoy the decorations!

- *Serve special treats for your customers.* A bank serves coffee and donut holes in its lobby every Saturday morning for its customers. Guess when most people in that town do their banking? Other organizations give special treats to the customers' children or even their dogs. The more unusual the treat, the more delighted the customer will be. Remember, however, that once you start this practice on a routine basis, the customers will come to *expect* it, and if it is not there for some reason, you will create unhappy customers!

- *Have a party for your customers.* You can make this event as involved as you choose, but the more planning and creativity you put into the party, the more memorable it will be and the more it will cement relationships and create loyal customers. You might have a "theme" day once a year and have all the employees come in costume. You might provide entertainment for your customers such as music or a fashion show or, better yet, a talent show that showcases your *own employees.*

- *Give your customers something free.* Everyone loves gifts! How many of us wait to buy our necessary cosmetics until they are having a "free gift with sale" promotion? The real challenge is to find a gift that is unique and represents your company or your mission in some creative way. If it is the same old thing, it will not delight your customers.

Nobody could clip coupons like Helen Struman.

Celebrate Individual Customers

When individual customers do business with you a certain number of times, celebrate them specially. Nowadays with computers we can track how many times a customer has purchased our product or used our service. Here are some ideas to trigger your thinking about thanking them for their business:

- When they have spent a certain amount of money with you, give them a coupon for a special savings. For example, some retail stores give you a coupon for $25 or $50 credit or a certain number of store credits after you have spent $500 or $1000 in their store.
- When they have used your service for the 25th or 50th or 100th time, make that service complimentary. For example, a limousine company gives the customer their 25th ride with them free, and a dry cleaner tracks the number of orders a customer has brought to them and gives them their 50th order for free.
- Ask each employee to write a thank-you note to one customer of his or her choice a week. You would be amazed at how much goodwill and loyalty this simple idea will create!

▶ TIPS FOR IMPLEMENTATION

Whatever you do, do it with class and sincerity. A tacky or cheap celebration is worse than none at all because it demonstrates that your customers are not really that important to you. And everyone in the organization needs to have the right attitude—that is, this time is special to appreciate and *enjoy* your customers, not resent having to spend extra time on them. Remember, they are the ones who bring you your paycheck!

51

Have a Thank Your Internal Customers Day

▶ **THE IDEA**

Very often we thank our external customers and yet we forget our internal ones. All the research shows that you will get employees to treat customers only as well as they are being treated themselves, so this is a time to celebrate and thank those internal people who make your work easier.

▶ **THE IDEA IN ACTION**

Every department in an organization has both internal customers and suppliers. Your internal customer is the person or department who needs *your* work in order to get their work done. For example, a customer service representative may turn in daily reports and account balances to the accounting or IT department. The people on those internal teams depend on those daily reports to be correct and timely in order to do their work, so they are the internal customers of the frontline customer service rep.

Which departments or individuals in your organization need your work in order to complete theirs? List some of your internal customers:

_____

_____

_____

_____

Not only do you have internal customers (other departments in your organization that need your work in order to do theirs), but you also are the customer of others within your organization. These departments or individuals are your supplier. A supplier is someone who provides quality products and services to an internal department or individual so they can complete their work accurately and on time.

Whose help do you need in order to complete your daily work? These departments or individuals are your suppliers. List some of your suppliers:

_____

_____

_____

_____

Now, once a quarter choose one of these groups of suppliers to your department and in some way honor them. Here are some ideas:

- Invite them to a potluck lunch.
- Bring them coffee and donuts in the morning.

**Although the other employees adored him,
Wayne the stockboy had a dark side.**

- Make a collage of your whole team's picture and have everyone sign it to thank them.
- Give them a fun mascot for their department that in some way symbolizes what they do for you; for example, give a stuffed salmon for the group that is "always swimming

upstream," a stuffed bee for the folks that "are always buzzing around," a frog for the department that always "hops to it," or a turtle because "they are always slow but sure."

- Have a team event—your team against their team—for friendly competition such as a Nerf baseball game in the parking lot or a Ping-Pong tournament or a "Who has the most beautiful baby/ grandchild / niece / nephew contest."

▶ TIPS FOR IMPLEMENTATION

Not only will celebrating your internal customers boost morale in your organization, but it will also provide teambuilding, fun, and understanding across the departments. Another idea that will really help in creating internal harmony is to have someone in your department trade jobs with someone in their department once a week. That way, individuals can fully understand and appreciate the dependence you have on each other. You might also choose to have a companywide appreciation day. Ken Butler, the Customer Services Manager for Philips Arena in Atlanta, just held a Mardi Gras theme party for 1200 staff to celebrate the end of a great year.

52

Add Your Personal Signature to Your Work

▶ **THE IDEA**

One of the ways you can express your sense of mission and the importance of your work is to find ways to put your personal stamp on all your interactions, whether they are in person or from "behind the scenes." It has been said that "every job is a self-portrait of the person who did it. Autograph your work with excellence." And, if your goal is to create loyal customers, add the words "Autograph your work with *excellence and caring!*" That will surprise and delight your customers and make your work much more fun.

▶ **THE IDEA IN ACTION**

Here are some examples of how other people have autographed their work:

- A nurse leaves a handwritten card by the bedside of her patients with a note introducing herself and assuring them of her care and understanding.
- A United Airlines pilot, after he gets things under control in the cockpit, goes to the computer and randomly selects the names of several passengers. He then handwrites short notes to them, thanking them for their business. When the flight attendant delivers them, it is a delightful surprise for all!
- A Northwest Airlines baggage attendant collects name tags that fall off luggage, and instead of throwing them away as they used to do, he mails them back to their owners.
- A taxi driver gives his customers a choice of five different kinds of music on cassette tapes as well as a variety of that day's newspapers to read. He also has a mission statement: "To get the customers to their destination as quickly, as safely, and as comfortably as possible!"
- An auto mechanic puts his card in every car he repairs. It reads, "This car cared for by [his name]."
- Paul Wilcox, former pastor of the First United Methodist Church in Harlan, Iowa, spends a great deal of his time visiting church members who are ill or shut-ins. To add a special, memorable sparkle to his visits, he brings his harmonica along and plays for his parishioners. When my mother had surgery recently, the second day he visited he first played "How Great Thou Art" to thank God for the success of the surgery and then, as my mother said, "He played a 'jazzier' tune" to boost her spirits!

- A vendor who owned a hot dog stand always asked the customer's name. His personal signature was to write their name in mustard on the hot dog!
- A state employee in Lansing, Michigan, writes personal notes on the back of personal checks such as "Merry Christmas," "The book was excellent!" or on utility bills, "Thanks for the warmth."
- If you enjoy funny sayings or quotations, you might consider sharing these with your customers, both internal and external. Some people have written a quotation on their business cards. I have a quote from Albert Schweitzer at the end of my résumé: "The only ones among us who will be truly happy are those who will have sought and found how to serve."
- One of the most touching examples of adding a personal signature is one of my signature stories that I tell each time I speak:

The Johnny Story

Recently I was asked to speak to 3000 employees of a large supermarket chain in the Midwest, an experience that led to one of the most heartwarming blessings of my entire speaking career. In this presentation I especially stressed the idea of adding a personal signature to your work.

About three weeks after I had spoken to the supermarket employees, my phone rang late one afternoon. The person on the line told me that his name was Johnny and that he was a bagger in one of the stores. He also told me that he was a Down's Syndrome person. He said, "Barbara, I liked what you said!" Then he went on to tell me how when he'd gone home that night, he asked his Dad to teach him to use the computer.

He said they set it up in three columns, and each night now when he goes home, he finds a "thought for the day." He said when he can't find one he likes, he "thinks one up"! Then he types it into the computer, prints them, cuts them out, and signs his name on the back of each one. The next day as he bags customers' groceries, "with flourish" he puts a thought for the day in each person's groceries he bags, adding his own personal signature in a heartwarming, fun, and creative way.

One month later the manager of the store called me. He said, "Barbara, you won't believe what happened today. . . . When I went out on the floor this morning, the line at Johnny's checkout was three times longer than any other line!" He said, "I went ballistic, yelling, 'Get more lanes open! Get more people out here,' but the customers said, 'No no! We want to be in Johnny's lane—we want the thought for the day!'"

He said one woman even came up and told him, "I only used to shop once a week, but now I come in every time I go by because I want the thought for the day!" (Imagine what that does to the bottom line.) He ended by saying, "Who do you think is the most important person in our whole store?"

Johnny, of course!

Three months later the manager called me again, "You and Johnny have transformed our store! Now in the floral department when they have a broken flower or an unused corsage, they go out on the floor and find an elderly woman or a little girl and pin it on them. One of our meat packers loves Snoopy, so he bought 50,000 Snoopy stickers, and each time he packages a piece of meat, he puts a Snoopy sticker on it. We are having so much fun, and our customers are having so much fun!" THAT is spirit in the workplace!"

Your personal signature is a declaration of your commitment to the quality of your work and to your customers. What creative ways can you think of to add your personal signature to your work?

▶ TIPS FOR IMPLEMENTATION

It never ceases to amaze me whenever I tell this beautiful story how little it takes to regenerate the spirit in a workplace and to delight the customers. Johnny took what many of us might consider to be a not-very-important job and he made it important by adding his own personal signature. My challenge and yours — *if young Johnny can do it, there is no reason why each one of us can't do it, too*. Imagine the new spirits of self-esteem, commitment, customer delight, and fun that could permeate our places of work if we each, like Johnny, found a way to add our special, unique touch to our job!

Conclusion

YOU HAVE A CHOICE!

Remember that you always have a choice! In all my work I speak and write about the concept of choice and how few people in our world today truly understand the choices they have. Instead, they see themselves as victims, always having an excuse or someone or something else to blame: "I can't do it because . . . "

One of the primary goals in my work is to help people "get in their gut" the belief that they *do* have choices. Several years ago I created the following simple chart to help me understand in a visual way the choices I have to make a difference every single day. This is true of every interaction you have with a customer, whether he or she is an internal or external customer.

I suggest that you give everyone in your organization a copy of this little chart that they can always keep with them as a reminder of the choice they have in *any* interaction—to create a minus, a zero, or a plus for that other person. For example, if you make the customer feel less important than you or your organization, that person will leave with a minus. If you simply take care of the business at hand but do not recognize the customer as a unique human being, the customer will leave with a zero. However, if you create a human-level connection, the customer will leave with a plus,

Your Choice in Every Interaction

Discounts (-)	Business Only (0)	Human-Level Connection (+)
	CHOICE	CHOICE

because a relationship was created. This connection can be as simple as using the person's name, giving her or him a compliment, or simply commenting on something outside of the working environment.

The bottom line is that each person *always has the choice* of whether or not he or she will create a positive interaction for the customer, regardless of how the customer is acting. And I believe this is the most important and empowering concept you can teach your employees.

Finally, if you are willing to implement one of the ideas in this book each week during the year, not only will you assure a continuous focus on customer service, but you will also have lots more fun in your workplace. Remember: *you will never get employees to treat customers any better than they are being treated themselves.* And most important of all, it is the little things that make a difference. Customers do not want the moon; they only want to be recognized as unique human beings with their own story.

Personal Responsiblity

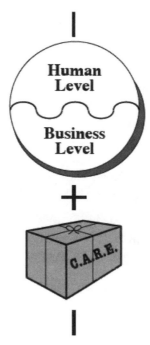

You <u>CAN</u> Make a Difference!

If you have ever received a CARE package, you remember what it felt like to have someone specially focus on you, and that is what each of you can do every single day with your customers. We all want so much more than to be treated as a number! Loyalty is created by how people feel in an interaction, and ultimately what turns us on and makes us come back is an *emotional attachment* to an organization. That emotional attachment begins with each person on your team.

May you be blessed as you reach out with CARE-ing to make a difference in the lives of your customers.

Warmly,

Barbara

6140 Midnight Pass Road #802
Sarasota, FL 34242
941-312-9169; Fax 941-349-8209
bglanz@barbaraglanz.com
www.barbaraglanz.com

Index

About the Author

Barbara Glanz, CSP (Certified Speaking Professional), works with organizations that want to improve morale, retention, and service and with people who want to rediscover the joy in their work and in their lives. She is the coauthor with Ken Blanchard of *The Simple Truths of Service as Inspired by Johnny the Bagger* and the author of

- *The Simple Truths of Appreciation: How Each of Us Can Choose to Make a Difference*
- *What Can I Do? Ideas to Help Those Who Have Experienced Loss*
- *180 Ways to Spread Contagious Enthusiasm*
- *Handle with CARE: Motivating and Retaining Employees*
- *Balancing Acts: More Than 250 Guiltfree, Creative Ideas to Blend Your Work and Your Life*
- *CARE Packages for the Workplace—Dozens of Little Things You Can Do to Regenerate Spirit at Work*
- *The Creative Communicator: 399 Ways to Make Your Business Communications Meaningful and Inspiring*

- *Building Customer Loyalty: How You Can Help Keep Customers Returning*
- *CARE Packages for the Home: Dozens of Ways to Regenerate Spirit Where You Live*

As an internationally known speaker, trainer, and consultant with a master's degree in Adult Education, Barbara lives and breathes her personal motto: "Spreading Contagious Enthusiasm." Since 1995, she has presented on all seven continents and in all 50 states to organizations as diverse as Nordstrom, Honda, the National Association for Employee Recognition, Southwest Airlines, Bank of America, USAA, Kaiser Permanente, Hallmark, the U.S. Department of Energy, Shangri-La Hotels, Merry Maids, Verizon, and the Singapore Security Police. You can reach her at bglanz@barbaraglanz.com or www.barbaraglanz.com. She lives on the beach in Sarasota, Florida, and delights in her grandchildren, Gavin, Kinsey, and Owen!